D1586980

*Managing Information*

# PROJECT PREPARATION

Published for
The National Examining Board for Supervisory Management

by
Pergamon Open Learning
*a division of*
Pergamon Press Ltd
Oxford · New York · Seoul · Tokyo

| U.K. | Pergamon Press Ltd, Headington Hill Hall, Oxford OX3 0BW, England |
| U.S.A. | Pergamon Press Inc, 660 White Plains Road, Tarrytown, New York 10591-513, USA |
| KOREA | Pergamon Press Korea, KPO Box 315, Seoul 110-603, Korea |
| JAPAN | Pergamon Press Japan, Tsunashima Building Annex, 3-20-12 Yushima, Bunkyo-ku, Tokyo 113, Japan |

This unit supersedes the Super Series first edition unit 305 (first edition 1987)

Second edition 1991
Reprinted 1992
Reprinted 1993

A catalogue record for this book is available from the British Library

ISBN book only: 0-08-041610-1

Design and Production: Pergamon Open Learning

NEBSM Project Manager: Pam Sear

Authors: Wendy & W. M. Payne
First Edition Authors: Wendy & W. M. Payne
Editor: Diana Thomas
Series Editor: Diana Thomas

Typeset by BPCC Techset Ltd, Exeter
Printed in Great Britain by BPCC Wheatons Ltd, Exeter

# CONTENTS

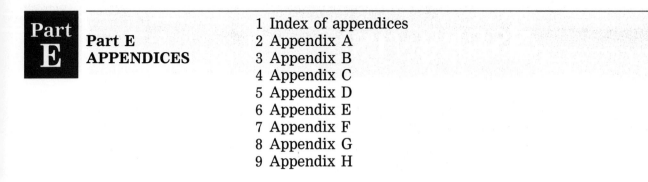

## 1    Welcome to the User Guide

Hello and welcome to the NEBSM Super Series second edition (Super Series 2) flexible training programme.

It is quite likely that you are a supervisor, a team leader, an assistant manager, a foreman, a section head, a first-line or a junior manager and have people working under you. The Super Series programme is ideal for all, whatever the job title, who are on or near that first rung of the management ladder. By choosing this programme we believe that you have made exactly the right decision when it comes to meeting your own needs and those of your organization.

The purpose of this guide is to help you gain the maximum benefit both from this particular workbook and also from a full supervisory management training programme.

You should read the whole of this User Guide thoroughly before you start any work on the unit and use the information and advice to help plan your studies.

If you are new to the idea of studying or training by yourself or have never before worked with a tutor or trainer on an individual basis, you should pay particular attention to the section below about Open Learning and tutorial support.

If you are a trainer or tutor evaluating this material for use with prospective students or clients, we think you will also find the information given here useful as it will help you to prepare and conduct individual pre-course counselling and group briefing sessions.

## 2    Your Open Learning Programme

**What do we mean by 'Open Learning'?**

Let's start by looking at what is meant by 'Open Learning' and how it could affect the way you approach your studies.

Open Learning is a term used to describe a method of training where you, the learner, make most of the decisions about *how*, *when* and *where* you do your learning. To make this possible you need to have available material, written or prepared in a special way (such as this book) and then have access to Open Learning centres that have been set up and prepared to offer guidance and support as and when required.

Undertaking your self-development training by Open Learning allows you to fit in with priorities at work and at home and to build the right level of confidence and independence needed for success, even though at first it may take you a little while to establish a proper routine.

**The workbook**

Though this guide is mainly aimed at you as a first time user, it is possible that you are already familiar with the earlier editions of the Super Series. If that is the case, you should know that there are quite a few differences in the workbook, some of which were very successfully trialled in the last 12 units of the first edition. Apart from the more noticeable features such as changes in page layouts and more extensive use of colour and graphics, you will find activities, questions and assignments that are more closely related to work and more thought-provoking.

In fact, there are so many extras now that are included as standard that the average study time per unit has been increased by almost a third. You will find a useful summary of all workbook features in the chart below and on page vii.

Whether you are a first time user or not, the first step towards being a successful Open Learner is to be familiar and comfortable with the learning material. It is well worth spending a little of your initial study time scanning the workbook to see how it is structured, what the various sections and features are called and what they are designed to do.

This will save you a lot of time and frustration when you start studying as you will then be able to concentrate on the actual subject matter itself without the need to refer back to what you are supposed to be doing with each part.

At the outset you are assumed to have no prior knowledge or experience of the subject and can expect to be taken logically, step by step from start to finish of the learning programme. To help you take on new ideas and information, and to help you remember and apply them, you will come across many different and challenging self check tasks, activities, quizzes and questions which you should approach seriously and enthusiastically. These features are designed not only to make your learning easier and more interesting but to help you to apply what you are studying to your own work situation in a practical and down-to-earth way.

To help to scan the workbook properly, and to understand what you find, here is a summary of the main features:

The workbook

| If you want: | Refer to: |
| --- | --- |
| An overview of every part of the workbook | The Unit map |
| A list of the main knowledge and skill outcomes you will gain from the unit | The Unit objectives |
| To check on your understanding of the subject and your progress as you work through each section | The Activities and Self checks |

Managing your
learning programme

When you feel you know your way around the material, and in particular appreciate the progress checking and assessment features, the next stage is to put together your own personal study plan and decide how best to study.

These two things are just as important as checking out the material; they are also useful time savers and give you the satisfaction of feeling organized and knowing exactly where you are going and what you are trying to achieve.

You have already chosen your subject (this unit) so you should now decide when you need to finish the unit and how much time you must spend to make sure you reach your target.

To help you to answer these questions, you should know that each workbook will probably take about *eight* to *ten* hours to complete; the variation in time allows for different reading, writing and study speeds and the length and complexity of any one subject.

Don't be concerned if it takes you longer than these average times, especially on your first unit, and always keep in mind that the objective of your training is understanding and applying the learning, not competing in a race.

Experience has shown that each unit is best completed over a two-week period with about *three* to *four* study hours spent on it in each week, and about *one* to *two* hours at each sitting. These times are about right for tackling a new subject and still keeping work and other commitments sensibly in balance.

Using these time guides you should set, and try to keep to, specific times, days, and dates for your study. You should write down what you have decided and keep it visible as a reminder. If you are studying more than one unit, probably as part of a larger training programme, then the compilation of a full, dated plan or schedule becomes even more important and might have to tie in with dates and times set by others, such as a tutor.

The next step is to decide where to study. If you are doing this training in conjunction with your company or organization this might be decided for you as most have quiet areas, training rooms, learning centres, etc., which you will be encouraged to use. If you are working at home, set aside a quiet corner where books and papers can be left and kept together with a comfortable chair and a simple writing surface. You will also need a note pad.

When you are finally ready to start studying, presuming that you are feeling confident and organized after your preparations, you should follow the instructions given in the Unit Map and the Unit Objectives pages.

You should work through each workbook section doing all that is asked of you until you reach the final assessments. Don't forget to keep your eye on the Unit Map as you progress and try to finish each session at a sensible point in the unit, ideally at the end of a complete section or part. You should always start your next session by looking back, for at least ten to fifteen minutes, at the work you did in the previous session.

You are encouraged to retain any reports, work-based assignments or other material produced in conjunction with your work through this unit in case you wish to present these later as evidence for a competency award or accreditation of prior learning.

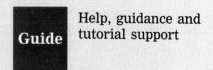

**Guide** | Help, guidance and tutorial support

The workbook has been designed to be as self-contained as possible, acting as your guide and tutor throughout your studies. However, there are bound to be times when you might not quite understand what the author is saying, or perhaps you don't agree with a certain point. Whatever the reason, we all need help and support from time to time and Open Learners are no exception.

Help during Open Learning study can come in many forms, providing you are prepared to seek it out and use it:

- first of all you could help yourself. Perhaps you are giving up too easily. Go back over it and try again;

- or you could ask your family or friends. Even if they don't understand the subject, the act of discussing it sometimes clarifies things in your own mind;

- then there is your company trainer or superior. If you are training as part of a company scheme, and during work time, then help and support will probably have been arranged for you already. Help and advice under these circumstances are important, especially as they can help you interpret your studies through actual and relevant company examples;

- if you are pursuing this training on your own, you could enlist expert help from a local Open Learning centre or agency. Such organizations exist in considerable numbers throughout the UK, often linked to colleges and other training establishments. The National Examining Board for Supervisory Management (NEBSM or NEBS Management), has several hundred such centres and can provide not only help and support but full assessment and accreditation facilities if you want to pursue a qualification as part of your chosen programme.

**3**     **The NEBSM Super Series 2**

The NEBSM Super Series second edition is a selection of workbook and audio cassette packages covering a wide range of supervisory and first line management topics.

Although the individual books and cassettes are completely self-contained and cover single subject areas, each belongs to one of the four modular groups shown. These groups can help you build up your personal development programme as you can easily see which subjects are related. The groups are also important if you undertake any NEBSM national award programme.

**Managing Human Resources**

| | | | |
|---|---|---|---|
| HR1 | Supervising at Work | HR10 | Managing Time |
| HR2 | Supervising with Authority | HR11 | Hiring People |
| HR3 | Team Leading | HR12 | Interviewing |
| HR4 | Delegation | HR13 | Training Plans |
| HR5 | Workteams | HR14 | Training Sessions |
| HR6 | Motivating People | HR15 | Industrial Relations |
| HR7 | Leading Change | HR16 | Employment and the Law |
| HR8 | Personnel in Action | HR17 | Equality at Work |
| HR9 | Performance Appraisal | HR18 | Work-based Assessment |

**Managing Information**

| | | | |
|---|---|---|---|
| IN1 | Communicating | IN7 | Using Statistics |
| IN2 | Speaking Skills | IN8 | Presenting Figures |
| IN3 | Orders and Instructions | IN9 | Introduction to Information Technology |
| IN4 | Meetings | | |
| IN5 | Writing Skills | IN10 | Computers and Communication Systems |
| IN6 | Project Preparation | | |

**Managing Financial Resources**

| | | | |
|---|---|---|---|
| FR1 | Accounting for Money | FR4 | Pay Systems |
| FR2 | Control via Budgets | FR5 | Security |
| FR3 | Controlling Costs | | |

**Managing Products and Services**

| | | | |
|---|---|---|---|
| PS1 | Controlling Work | PS8 | Productivity |
| PS2 | Health and Safety | PS9 | Stock Control Systems |
| PS3 | Accident Prevention | PS10 | Stores Control |
| PS4 | Ensuring Quality | PS11 | Efficiency in the Office |
| PS5 | Quality Techniques | PS12 | Marketing |
| PS6 | Taking Decisions | PS13 | Caring for the Environment |
| PS7 | Solving Problems | PS14 | Caring for the Customer |

While the contents have been thoroughly updated, many Super Series 2 titles remain the same as, or very similar to the first edition units. Where, through merger, rewrite or deletion title changes have also been made, this summary should help you. If you are in any doubt please contact Pergamon Open Learning direct.

**First Edition**

Merged titles
105 Organization Systems and 106 Supervising in the System
100 Needs and Rewards and 101 Enriching Work
502 Discipline and the Law and 508 Supervising and the Law
204 Easy Statistics and 213 Descriptive Statistics
200 Looking at Figures and 202 Using Graphs
210 Computers and 303 Communication Systems

402 Cost Reduction and 405 Cost Centres
203 Method Study and 208 Value Analysis

Major title changes
209 Quality Circles
205 Quality Control

Deleted titles
406 National Economy/410 Single European Market

**Second Edition**

HR1 Supervising at Work
HR6 Motivating People
HR16 Employment and the Law
IN7 Using Statistics
IN8 Presenting Figures
IN10 Computers and Communication Systems
FR3 Controlling Costs
PS8 Productivity

PS4 Ensuring Quality
PS5 Quality Techniques

The NEBSM Super Series 2 Open Learning material is published by Pergamon Open Learning in conjunction with NEBS Management.

NEBS Management is the largest provider of management education, training courses and qualifications in the United Kingdom, operating through over 700 Centres. Many of these Centres offer Open Learning and can provide help to individual students.

Many thousands of students follow the Open Learning route with great success and gain NEBSM or other qualifications.

NEBSM maintains a twin track approach to Supervisory Management training offering knowledge-based awards at three levels:

● the NEBSM Introductory Award in Supervisory Management;
● the NEBSM Certificate in Supervisory Management;
● the NEBSM Diploma in Supervisory Management;

and competence based awards at two levels:

● the NEBSM NVQ in Supervisory Management at Level 3;
● the NEBSM NVQ in Management at Level 4.

**Knowledge-based awards and Super Series 2**

The ***Introductory Award*** requires a minimum of 30 hours of study and provides a grounding in the theory and practice of supervisory management. An agreed programme of up to five NEBSM Super Series 2 units plus a one-day workshop satisfactorily completed can lead to this Award. Pre-approved topic combinations exist for general, industrial and commercial options. Completed Super Series 2 units can be allowed as an exemption towards the full NEBSM Certificate.

The ***Certificate in Supervisory Management*** requires study of up to 23 NEBSM Super Series 2 units and participation in group activity or workshops. The assessment system includes work-based assignments, a case study, a project and an oral interview. The certificate is divided into four modules and each one may be completed separately.
A ***Module Award*** can be made on successful completion of each module, and when the assessments are satisfactorily completed the Certificate is awarded. Students will need to register with a NEBSM Centre in order to enter for an award; NEBSM can advise you.

The ***Diploma in Supervisory Management*** consists of the formulation and implementation of a Personal Development Plan plus a generic management core. The programme is assessed by means of a log book, case study/in tray exercises, project or presentation.

The NEBSM Super Series 2 Open Learning material is designed for use at Certificate level but can also be used for the Introductory Award and provide valuable background knowledge for the Diploma.

| Competence-based programmes and Super Series 2 | The ***NEBSM NVQ in Supervisory Management Level 3*** is based upon the seven units of competence produced by the Management Charter Initiative (MCI) in their publication *Supervisory Management Standards* of June 1992. It is recognized by the National Council for Vocational Qualifications (NCVQ) at Level 3 in their framework. |

The ***NEBSM NVQ in Management Level 4*** is based upon the nine units of competence produced by MCI in their publication *Occupational Standards for Managers, Management 1 and Assessment Criteria* of April 1991. It is recognized by the National Council for Vocational Qualifications (NCVQ) at Level 4 in their framework.

Super Series 2 units can be used to provide the necessary underpinning knowledge, skills and understanding that are required to prepare yourself for competence-based assessment.

Working through Super Series 2 units cannot, by itself, provide you with everything you need to enter or be entered for competence assessment. This must come from a combination of skill, experience and knowledge gained both on and off the job.

You will also find many of the 47 Super Series 2 units of use in learning programmes for other National Vocational Qualifications (NVQs) which include elements of supervisory management. Please check with the relevant NVQ lead body for information on Units of Competence and underlying knowledge, skills and understanding.

| Competence Match Chart | The Competence Match Chart overleaf illustrates which Super Series 2 titles provide background vital to the current MCI M1S Supervisory Management Standards. You will also find that there is similar matching at MCI M1, Management 1 Standards. This is shown on the chart on page xiii. |

For more information about MCI contact:

Management Charter Initiative
Russell Square House
10–12 Russell Square
London
WC1B 5BZ

| Progression | Many successful NEBSM students use their qualifications as stepping stones to other awards, both educational and professional. Recognition is given by a number of bodies for this purpose. Further details about this and other NEBSM matters can be obtained from: |

NEBSM Information Officer
The National Examining Board for Supervisory Management
76 Portland Place
London
W1N 4AA

The chart shows matches of Super Series 2 titles with MCI M1S (Supervisory Management) Units of Competence. Titles indicated ● are directly relevant to MCI Units, those marked ◐ provide specific supporting information, and those listed ○ provide useful general background.

| | NEBSM Super Series 2 Titles | 1 | 2 | 3 | 4 | 5 | 6 | 7 |
|---|---|---|---|---|---|---|---|---|
| PS1 | Controlling Output | ◐ | ◐ | | | | | |
| PS2 | Health and Safety | ● | ○ | | | ○ | | |
| PS3 | Accident Prevention | ● | ○ | | | ○ | | |
| PS4 | Ensuring Quality | ● | ○ | | | | | |
| PS5 | Quality Techniques | ● | | | | | | |
| PS6 | Taking Decisions | ○ | ○ | | | ◐ | ◐ | |
| PS7 | Solving Problems | ○ | ○ | | | ◐ | ● | |
| PS8 | Productivity | | ◐ | | | ● | | |
| PS9 | Stock Control Systems | | ◐ | | | | | |
| PS10 | Stores Control | | ◐ | | | | | |
| PS11 | Efficiency in the Office | | ◐ | | | ◐ | | |
| PS12 | Marketing | ○ | | | | | | |
| PS13 | Caring for the Environment | ◐ | ◐ | | | ○ | ○ | ○ |
| PS14 | Caring for the Customer | ◐ | ○ | | | ○ | | |
| HR1 | Supervising at Work | | | | | ● | ● | |
| HR2 | Supervising with Authority | | | | | ● | ● | |
| HR3 | Team Leading | | | | | ● | ● | |
| HR4 | Delegation | | | | ● | ● | ◐ | |
| HR5 | Workteams | | | | | ● | ● | |
| HR6 | Motivating People | | | | | ● | ● | |
| HR7 | Leading Change | | ◐ | | | ● | | |
| HR8 | Personnel in Action | | | ● | | | | |
| HR9 | Performance Appraisal | | | | ● | | ● | |
| HR10 | Managing Time | | | ○ | ○ | | | |
| HR11 | Hiring People | | | ● | | | | |
| HR12 | Interviewing | | | ● | ● | ◐ | ● | |
| HR13 | Training Plans | | | | ● | | | |
| HR14 | Training Sessions | | | | ● | | | |
| HR15 | Industrial Relations | | | | | | ● | |
| HR16 | Employment and the Law | | | ○ | | | ● | |
| HR17 | Equality at Work | | | ◐ | | | ● | |
| HR18 | Work-based Assessment | | | ○ | ● | ● | ○ | ○ |
| FR1 | Accounting for Money | | ● | | | | | |
| FR2 | Control via Budgets | | ● | | | | | |
| FR3 | Controlling Costs | | ● | | | | | |
| FR4 | Pay Systems | | | | | | | |
| FR5 | Security | ◐ | ◐ | | | | | |
| IN1 | Communicating | ○ | ○ | ○ | ○ | ○ | ○ | ● |
| IN2 | Speaking Skills | ○ | ○ | ○ | ○ | ○ | ○ | ● |
| IN3 | Orders and Instructions | ◐ | | | | ● | ● | |
| IN4 | Meetings | | | | ○ | ● | ◐ | ● |
| IN5 | Writing Skills | ○ | ◐ | | ○ | ◐ | ○ | ● |
| IN6 | Project Preparation | | | | ○ | | | |
| IN7 | Using Statistics | ◐ | ◐ | | | | | ● |
| IN8 | Presenting Figures | ◐ | ◐ | | | | | ● |
| IN9 | Introduction to Information Technology | ◐ | ◐ | | | | | ● |
| IN10 | Computers and Communication Systems | ◐ | ◐ | | | | | ● |

**\* MCI M1 S  Units of Competence**

1. Maintain services and operations to meet quality standards
2. Contribute to the planning, monitoring and control of resources
3. Contribute to the provision of personnel
4. Contribute to the training and development of teams, individuals and self to enhance performance
5. Contribute to the planning, organization and evaluation of work
6. Create, maintain and enhance productive working relationships
7. Provide information and advice for action towards meeting organizational objectives

**Competence Match Chart MCI M1**

The chart indicates the Super Series 2 titles which provide some useful background information to support MCI M1 (Management level 1) Units of Competence.

**NEBSM Super Series 2 Titles**     **MCI M1 Units of Competence (see below\*)**

| | | 1 | 2 | 3 | 4 | 5 | 6 | 7 | 8 | 9 |
|---|---|---|---|---|---|---|---|---|---|---|
| PS1 | Controlling Output | △ | △ | | | | | | | |
| PS2 | Health and Safety | △ | | | | | | | | |
| PS3 | Accident Prevention | △ | | | | | | | | |
| PS4 | Ensuring Quality | △ | △ | | | | | | | |
| PS5 | Quality Techniques | △ | △ | | | | | | | |
| PS6 | Taking Decisions | | | | | | | | △ | △ |
| PS7 | Solving Problems | | △ | | | | | | △ | △ |
| PS8 | Productivity | | △ | | | | | | | |
| PS9 | Stock Control Systems | △ | | | | | | | | |
| PS10 | Stores Control | △ | | | | | | | | |
| PS11 | Efficiency in the Office | △ | △ | | | | | | | |
| PS12 | Marketing | △ | | | | | | | | |
| PS13 | Caring for the Environment | △ | | | | | | | | |
| PS14 | Caring for the Customer | | △ | | | | | | | |
| HR1 | Supervising at Work | | | | | | | △ | | |
| HR2 | Supervising with Authority | | | | | | | △ | | △ |
| HR3 | Team Leading | | | | | △ | △ | △ | | |
| HR4 | Delegation | | | | | △ | △ | △ | | |
| HR5 | Workteams | | | | | △ | △ | △ | | △ |
| HR6 | Motivating People | | | | | | | △ | | |
| HR7 | Leading Change | | △ | | | | | | | |
| HR8 | Personnel in Action | | | | △ | | | | | |
| HR9 | Performance Appraisal | | | | | | | △ | | |
| HR10 | Managing Time | | | | | | | | | |
| HR11 | Hiring People | | | | △ | | | | | |
| HR12 | Interviewing | | | | △ | △ | | △ | | |
| HR13 | Training Plans | | | | △ | | | | | |
| HR14 | Training Sessions | | | | △ | | | | | |
| HR15 | Industrial Relations | | | | | | | △ | | |
| HR16 | Employment and the Law | | | | △ | | | △ | | |
| HR17 | Equality at Work | | | | △ | | | △ | | |
| HR18 | Work-based Assessment | | | | | △ | △ | | | |
| FR1 | Accounting for Money | | | △ | | | | | | |
| FR2 | Control via Budgets | | | △ | | | | | | |
| FR3 | Controlling Costs | | | △ | | | | | | |
| FR4 | Pay Systems | | | | | | | | | |
| FR5 | Security | | | | | | | | | |
| IN1 | Communicating | | | | | | | △ | | △ |
| IN2 | Speaking Skills | | | △ | | | | △ | | △ |
| IN3 | Orders and Instructions | | | | | | | △ | | △ |
| IN4 | Meetings | | | | | | | △ | | △ |
| IN5 | Writing Skills | | | △ | | | △ | △ | | △ |
| IN6 | Project Preparation | | | △ | | | △ | △ | | |
| IN7 | Using Statistics | | | | | | △ | △ | △ | |
| IN8 | Presenting Figures | | | | | | △ | △ | | △ |
| IN9 | Introduction to Information Technology | | | | | | | | △ | △ |
| IN10 | Computers and Communication Systems | | | | | | | | △ | △ |

**\* MCI M1 Units of Competence**

Key Role: Manage Operations —
1. Maintain and improve service and product operations
2. Contribute to the implementation of change in services, products and systems

Key Role: Manage Finance —
3. Recommend, monitor and control the use of resources

Key Role: Manage People —
4. Contribute to the recruitment and selection of personnel
5. Develop teams, individuals and self to enhance performance
6. Plan, allocate and evaluate work carried out by teams, individuals and self
7. Create, maintain and enhance effective working relationships

Key Role: Manage Information —
8. Seek, evaluate and organise information for action
9. Exchange information to solve problems and make decisions

**Guide** | Unit Completion Certificate

Completion of this Certificate by an authorized and qualified person indicates that you have worked through all parts of this unit and completed all assessments. If you are studying this unit as part of a certificated programme, or think you may wish to in future, then completion of this Certificate is particularly important as it may be used for exemptions, credit accumulation or Accreditation of Prior Learning (APL). Full details can be obtained from NEBSM.

---

**NEBSM SUPER SERIES Second Edition**

*IN6*

*Project Preparation*

. . . . . . . . . . . . . . . . . . . . . . . . . . .

*has satisfactorily completed this unit.*

*Name of Signatory* . . . . . . . . . . . . . . .

*Position* . . . . . . . . . . . . . . . . . . . . . . .

*Signature* . . . . . . . . . . . . . . . . . . . . . .

*Date* . . . . . . . .

*Official Stamp*

---

Keep in touch

Pergamon Open Learning and NEBS Management are always happy to hear of your experiences of using the Super Series to help improve supervisory and managerial effectiveness. This will assist us with continuous product improvement, and novel approaches and success stories may be included in promotional information to illustrate to others what can be done.

## 1      Unit map

**WORKBOOK**

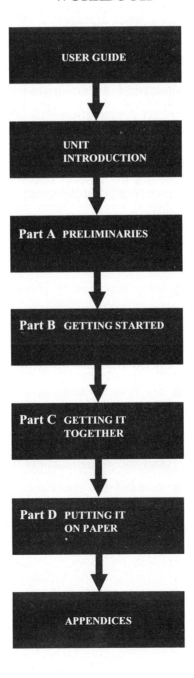

USER GUIDE

UNIT INTRODUCTION

Part A  PRELIMINARIES

Part B  GETTING STARTED

Part C  GETTING IT TOGETHER

Part D  PUTTING IT ON PAPER

APPENDICES

Investigating problems and situations and searching for solutions is all part of everyday supervisory management. On a day-to-day basis many such situations are usually resolved straight away or within a very short period of time and without too much time and effort.

There are occasions, however, when such problems and situations are much larger, more complex and more long term and require specific time, resources and skills to be set aside, for example when the office has to be completely reorganized or problems with the quality of a new piece of equipment have to be resolved. When this is necessary we refer to them as 'projects' or 'assignments' or some similar name which tells us that, by their length and complexity they are something different. Projects *always* require a fully comprehensive written report at the end, summarizing all the findings and recommendations.

To acquire the knowledge and skill to undertake such projects properly and to communicate the results both in a spoken and written way is extremely useful for you as a supervisor or manager, especially as you can never quite be sure when such skills are likely to be called upon. And it wouldn't do to have to reply that you don't know what a project is or how to go about it.

NEBS Management also believe that effective execution of a project is an important skill for supervisors and managers to acquire and develop, which is why they include the project in their Supervisory Management Certificate course as part of the assessments.

*Project Preparation* will help you in two ways. It will give you all the information, help and guidance required to recognize and undertake with confidence any size and type of work-based project, assignment or extended report, *and* it will tell you all you need to know about meeting the project requirements of the NEBSM Certificate in Supervisory Management should you be following that course of study.

**In this unit we will:**

● define what is meant by a project and give examples;

● show how you go about selecting a project for investigation;

● detail how we agree and set the project boundaries and produce something called the Terms of Reference;

● examine techniques and good practice for gathering information about the current situation;

● see how to analyze collected data and to produce solutions and recommendations;

● show you how to write a project report that is not only an effective piece of communication but one that actually *sells* those solutions and recommendations to a reader;

● examine the specific requirements of the NEBSM project as part of the Certificate in Supervisory Management assessment criteria.

**Objectives**

On completion of this unit you should be *better able to*:

● select and define a situation or problem for investigation (a project);

● gather all the relevant facts;

● analyse those facts and draw conclusions;

● write a report and make recommendations;

● meet the project requirements of the NEBSM Certificate in Supervisory Management.

# PRELIMINARIES

## 1 First thoughts

Here are some thoughts to mull over at the time when you are just beginning to think about undertaking a project. They will help you to get 'tuned in' so that you will benefit from the challenge of a project and enjoy the experience.

*Why* is the satisfactory completion of a project one of the requirements for the award of a NEBSM Certificate?

*Because* satisfactory completion of the project demonstrates the following.

● You were willing to commit yourself and persevere.

● You were able to:

  – plan and organize a task;

  – carry a task through to the end;

  – use initiative/imagination/originality.

● You knew, or have learned, how to:

  – collect facts and evidence;

  – analyze;

  – think logically;

  – solve a problem;

  – communicate.

The project gives you the opportunity to integrate ideas from different parts of the NEBSM syllabus and apply them in a practical situation. Do not think of it as just a testing device. It is a learning situation. At the end of a project you will know a lot more about the subject or topic. You will know a lot more about how to tackle a problem, *and* you will have learned a considerable amount about people – especially yourself.

This is useful 'under the belt' experience for any supervisory manager.

## 2 Sources of help

There will be times when you feel totally alone and isolated. This feeling has been experienced by almost everyone who has carried out a worthwhile project. You need to know where and to whom you can turn for help, guidance and encouragement. Do not try to soldier on alone.

**2.1 Senior colleagues/ experts in your organization**

Is there someone who has looked at a similar problem or who has specialized knowledge and can point you in the right direction? Do not be afraid of approaching a senior person. There are very few people who will turn their backs on a request for help or advice.

**2.2 NEBSM Centres**

The difficulty you face at any point may be very similar to one which the NEBSM course tutor helped someone else to overcome last week or last month. NEBSM places importance on the role played by the course tutor in helping people to achieve good project standards.

**2.3**
**This study unit**

As we said earlier, this unit can be used twice: once to learn how to tackle a project, then a second time as a memory jogger when you are working on your actual project. Apart from the text there is additional information in the Appendices. Look down the contents page and see what might be applicable to your particular query.

**2.4**
**Trained librarians**

If your problem relates to finding information, seek out a librarian. Go to your local reference library, or the library of the NEBSM centre.

Many librarians are top sleuths at digging out information. They can lead you not only to books but to pamphlets, digests, specialized journals. They will turn to directories, abstracts and publication lists to find references to a particular industry, subject or printed article. Their skill in tracing information can be of tremendous help to anyone carrying out a project. Their doggedness in tracking down information is an example the project first-timer should learn from!

## 3         Practicalities

**3.1**
**Clearing the decks for action**

There are some people who are able to start *any* task straight away. Others suffer from what is called a 'tidy my desk' syndrome.

'I can't paper the landing because I need to repair the attic trap-door first.'

'I can't dig the garden until I've turned out the shed.'

'I can't write this letter until I've sorted these papers on the desk.'

*Stop* making excuses. The sure-fire way to enjoy work is to *do* it and get it done!

*Start* by creating the basis for self-discipline.

You will need:

● materials for making notes;

● somewhere to keep the information you accumulate;

● an established work-base.

**3.2**
**For making notes**

● A spiral-bound reporter's notebook: handy to carry; sheets flip over easily; easy to tear out sheet to hand a note to someone or leave a note for yourself or to store when it has been actioned (be extravagant – to make life easier don't deal with more than one type of information on any sheet).

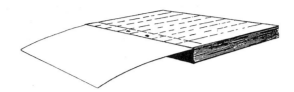

● A pad of lined paper, A4 size: gets you used to A4 so it will help you to visualize later on what a particular page of your finished project will look like; usually has holes ready punched; available in narrow- or broad-spaced lines. (Disadvantage: not so handy to carry around unless you have a brief-case with you.)

● Small index cards (not smaller than 6″ × 4″): a handy way of gathering information (one item to a card) – you always carry two or three blank cards with you for odd ideas and jottings; cards are useful for sorting and sifting your information into sections and for signalling reminders to yourself – for instance, a red X in a corner could mean letter to be written (or phone call to be made or whatever), a corner cut off could mean the card was complete with no further action needed until the writing stage.

**3.3**
**For storage**

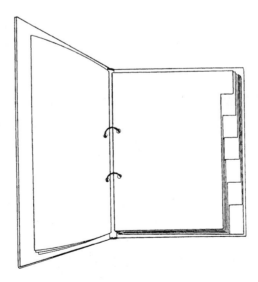

● A loose-leaf folder, A4 size with spring rings and dividers: keeps all your notes together irrespective of paper size; dividers can be labelled, and relabelled if you find your first ideas on the divisions don't work.

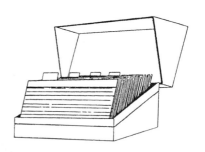

● Storage box with dividers for 6″ × 4″ index cards: a very compact way of gathering information together. Often only alphabetical dividers can be found, which may not be how you want to work, but the backs are plain so turn them around to make your own division headings.

● As well as your own notes and jottings, you may find it necessary to accumulate leaflets, brochures, lists, computer print-outs, etc. So consider which of the following may be right for you:

– a wallet-type cardboard file, or expanding file, or box file;

– a number of large envelopes that you can label appropriately;

– a spare brief-case or attaché case;

– an empty desk drawer or filing-cabinet drawer or any other suitable enclosed space which can be used *exclusively* for project matters.

**3.4**
**Other tools you**
**may need**

| pens | pencils | coloured pens |
|------|---------|---------------|
| ruler | squared paper | graph paper |
| calculator | stapler | hole-punch |
| bull-dog clips | Acco fasteners | treasury tags |

**3.5**
**A work-base**

Establish one spot as your work-base. Use one particular chair and one particular table or desk. The human brain works on a 'patterning' process. You create a pattern by using this one spot consistently. When you sit down to work on your project your mind is already focusing on the matter and you will find it easier to concentrate each time you start.

## 4    The size of it

A question many people ask is 'How long must the report be?'

At this stage this is not a good question to ask. If someone asked how many miles they must travel before they can pass a driving-test, the answer would have to be 'Enough!' The same answer applies to the project, because the report sets out what you have *done*.

**Project Danger Warning**

Early obsession with the writing *can hinder the investigation.*

In Part B you will consider how detailed your investigation is to be. You will be setting the size of the *project*. From that will evolve how long the written report will be. It must not be padded out to make it look weighty or to reach a specified number of words.

Probably there is now a different question in your mind: 'How big must a NEBSM project be?'

A worthwhile project which has been properly investigated is unlikely to be written up in less than 3,000 words. However, effective use of charts and photographs can reduce this number. But do not take *too* literally a maxim you may have heard: 'One picture is worth a thousand words'. The assessor expects to see more than three pictures!

What *does* an assessor look for?

See Appendix A 'What an assessor looks for'.

To visualize words on A4 paper, this may help:

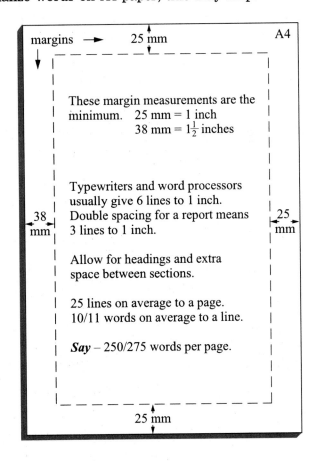

margins → 25 mm      A4

These margin measurements are the minimum.   25 mm = 1 inch
38 mm = $1\frac{1}{2}$ inches

Typewriters and word processors usually give 6 lines to 1 inch. Double spacing for a report means 3 lines to 1 inch.

Allow for headings and extra space between sections.

25 lines on average to a page.
10/11 words on average to a line.

*Say* – 250/275 words per page.

38 mm      25 mm

25 mm

## 1 Choosing a project

NEBSM encourages practical, down-to-earth supervisory management training. Therefore your project should deal with a practical subject, work-based if possible.

The problem or situation you are to investigate should have supervisory management aspects and not be entirely technical.

## Activity 1

> ■ Time guide 2 minutes
>
> Look at the project topics below and think what type of problems are involved. Write down against each the letter T if you think it is a technical problem and the letter M if you think it is a management problem.
>
> 1 The design of a piece of apparatus or equipment _____
>
> 2 The planning and layout for a process _____
>
> 3 The change from total shut-down summer break to staggered holidays _____

Did you write T for the first? The word 'design' rather implies that the first is a technical project – for engineering students, perhaps – not really a NEBSM project.

How about the second? I thought it could be T *or* M or both T *and* M. It might be something which entailed only technical considerations, but on the other hand, planning is a management function and layout can affect efficiency and may involve people: these are certainly management aspects.

Number three is definitely M. A major change such as this would entail evaluation, planning, organizing and very careful communication: certainly a project with many management considerations.

A work-based practical project can also be in an *employer's* interests. In a busy workplace there may be matters that are not serious enough to have reached the top of management's priority list. Yet they do need attention, and that means time.

You will be *making* time for your project – your own time. Your employer benefits from this, but you also gain a benefit – the help and support of your organization.

## 2 Know what your project is

First things first: before plunging into your project, know what your project is.

This may sound crazy, but people have been known to start without having a clear target in mind. This wastes a lot of time and causes a great deal of frustration.

To give you an idea of the sort of thing that can happen, let's take a look at what's going on in the studio.

| Players: | Bob Bumbler, *Manager*<br>Joe Soap, *Supervisor* |
|---|---|
| *Bob:* | Come in, Joe, sit yourself down. What's the problem? |
| *Joe:* | I've come about my project. Remember, you said you'd settle what I'm to do. |
| *Bob:* | Ah yes... um... well, Joe, I've given the matter a lot of thought and... er... um... we... er... need you to do something that's not only good for you but good for the firm... |
| *Joe:* | Great. I'm so glad you've come up with something because I just didn't know what to do. |
| *Bob:* | No problem, Joe. Now... um... What was it I had in mind?... er... um... layout, that's it, layout... |
| *Joe:* | Layout? |
| *Bob:* | Yes, layout. Space. You know, ...the whole area we work in. It all costs the firm money. Are we getting good value for it? ... er ... Do we use it to the best advantage? All that sort of thing. |
| *Joe:* | Oh I see: a kind of survey of the property you mean? |
| *Bob:* | That's it, Joe, a survey of layout. Just the job for your project. |
| *Joe:* | Thanks, Bob. I knew you'd sort something out. Layout seems a good idea. |
| *Bob:* | Fine. That's settled then. Layout. I'll look forward to reading it. Hey! I'll even throw in a title for you. 'Layout – are we getting good value? Now, I must get on... bit pressured today, you know how it is... |
| *Joe:* | Yes, I know how it is, Bob. Thanks for your time. |

I wonder what you feel about what has just taken place in the manager's office? It seems to me that Joe Soap is the sort of chap who will go home, get a clean sheet of paper and write at the top 'Layout – are we getting good value?' And then stop, and wonder, and flounder.

From experience, I should say that whatever efforts he may make are doomed to failure. 'Death by Waffle' might be a more appropriate title!

You may think that no one could be daft enough to start a project on such an ill-defined base. But project tutors will confirm that it happens – and not just on rare occasions. Project disasters are based on waffle and woolly thinking!

Look at Scene 1 more closely. Bumbler said he'd given the matter a lot of thought. Do you believe this? Note how he waffles on whilst he scrabbles around for an idea.

'Layout,' he cries, and burbles on about costs, space, value, best advantage, trying to cover up for the lack of thought given to Joe's project.

Bob Bumblers abound. They lead people like Joe into writing 'Layout – are we getting good value?' at the top of a page and thinking that they are on the right road to a first-class project.

**2.1**
**Two guidelines**

Here are two guidelines to help you to **know what your project is.**

● Establish the topic/subject.

● Establish the parameters.

We'll look at each of these guidelines in more detail.

Guideline 1:

Establish the topic/subject

You must be totally clear in your own mind what you setting out to do. The precise terms of a project can be quite hard to settle, but it is essential to know what it is you are tackling.

Let's have an Action Replay of Scene 1, but this time we shall see Sam Sharp instead of Joe.

A manager's office

| *Players:* | *Bob Bumbler, Manager* |
| | *Sam Sharp, Supervisor* |

*(Fade in on Bob as he makes his layout 'face-saver' speech)*

| *Bob:* | ... What was it I had in mind? ... er ... layout, that's it, layout ... |
| *Sam:* | Layout of what? |
| *Bob:* | Space ... you know what I mean ... the ... er ... um ... whole area we work in. |
| *Sam:* | What about it? |
| *Bob:* | Well, it costs the firm money, doesn't it? Are we making the most of it? |
| *Sam:* | You mean you'd like me to have a look at how we make use of the space we've got and see if we could do better? |
| *Bob:* | Got it in one, Sam. Make an excellent project for you and be good for the firm too ... |
| *Sam:* | That could be a good idea, Bob, but it needs a bit of thinking about. Tell you what: let me give it some thought, then come back to you. |

| *Bob:* | Fine, Sam, do that. Now, I must get on . . . bit pressured today, you know how it is . . . |
| *Sam:* | I know exactly how it is, Bob. |

Obviously Sam is sharper than Joe. His two short questions cut across waffle. The replies to them confirm Sam's suspicion that no thought has been given to the project subject. He tells Bob his idea is good, and suggests another meeting.

Bumbler is off the hook. Sam has time to gather his thoughts.

Whilst Joe is writing down his project title (raring to go down to Disasterville), Sam is quietly thinking about Bumbler's waffle idea. What was in Bob's mind? Anything or nothing? There could be merit in looking at how the firm makes use of space, but he must have something more definite to get his teeth into.

How does Sam go about this? He starts off by writing down a list of possibilities. Could it be:

● where machines or racks are positioned?

● work-flow in a specific area, or in all areas?

● where people are in relation to the work they do or to each other?

● the convenience or otherwise of the present set-up?

● making space for possible expansion?

Sam lets his thoughts simmer for a day or so. He knows he has to figure out some specific questions for his next meeting. That way both he and Bob will know what is to be undertaken.

## Activity 2

■ Time guide 3 minutes

Choose **one** of the possibilities that Sam has written down. Write down **two** questions you would ask that would help to establish the parameters.

_____

_____

_____

_____

There are various ways in which you could have phrased your questions. Certainly one question would need to establish just what area of the company's buildings is to be considered.

The main thing is to look at your questions and see if they would bring answers that would clarify the bounds of the project. Questions that have a specific focus are more likely to result in specific answers.

This is how Sam coped with **his** situation.

A manager's office

**Case Study**

| | |
|---|---|
| *Players:* | *Bob Bumbler, Manager*<br>*Sam Sharp, supervisor* |

Time: two days later

| | |
|---|---|
| *Bob:* | Come in, Sam. What can I do for you? |
| *Sam:* | It's about that idea you had for my project. |
| *Bob:* | Ah, yes, your project . . . er, just remind me where we'd got to, Sam. |
| *Sam:* | Layout – use of space: that's what you said. Well, I thought it worth developing a bit and then seeing what you think. |
| *Bob:* | Good. So, what are your ideas? |
| *Sam:* | Well, this is a big place. I reckon I should stick to those areas I know something about. At least I have a sound experience of the two main workshops – B and C – and maybe I could also look at E as well. |
| *Bob:* | Sounds reasonable. So what's the problem? |
| *Sam:* | But what am I actually looking at? How equipment is positioned in relation to the work-flow or what? |
| *Bob:* | Does it matter? |
| *Sam:* | It matters to me: this project has got to be assessed. It should have some specific angle. |
| *Bob:* | You've had more time to think this out than I have, Sam, so I'm just listening. |
| *Sam:* | Fine, then can we have cards on the table, Bob? |
| *Bob:* | Sure, go ahead. |
| *Sam:* | Well, rumour has it the firm is thinking of expanding production and . . . |
| *Bob:* | Rumour, just rumour . . . nothing official . . . I've said nothing . . . but do go on. |
| *Sam:* | OK, a nod is as good as a wink. Suppose I look into the present production methods in B and C workshops with the idea of seeing if productivity can be improved with existing resources? And I've said nothing either. |
| *Bob:* | I like it, Sam. Think you can make a job of it? |
| *Sam:* | Yes, with a bit of support from you. But if my project is to be any good I realize that a lot of the information I get may have to be kept under wraps. |
| *Bob:* | I'll have to get the OK from the old man first – the situation is a bit tricky. |
| *Sam:* | Well, you know I can keep my trap shut. |
| *Bob:* | Look, give me a couple days to get clearance and then come back to me. I'd like you to do this project, Sam. It needs doing. |
| *Sam:* | Let's hope the old man is enthusiastic too. I've got to make a good job of my project or I goof the whole course. |

From this conversation it seems likely that when Bob originally grabbed at the layout idea it was because the expansion scheme was in his mind, but this was a confidential matter. Sam had carefully thought through the loose, waffle idea and prepared his questions. Thus he has managed to clarify the subject of his project. It now has meaning and purpose.

Provided the 'old man' gives the go-ahead, Sam is in a much better position to achieve a worthwhile project report than poor Joe Soap, who started out without knowing where he was going!

Guideline 2:     Establish the parameters

The parameters are:

- *firstly*, the boundaries in terms of space or things;

    For instance, are you to look at:

    - one department (office, ward, section) or several departments?

    - one product or a number of products?

    - one area or all areas?

    - one make of machines or alternative makes?

- *secondly*, the limits in terms of time;

    These are some of the questions to which you may need to find the answers.

    - How long will the fact-finding take?

    - How far back should the investigation go?

    - What is an adequate period to survey?

    - When is the new system/equipment/staff needed?

    - When is the final written report due?

- *thirdly*, any 'no go' areas.

    Certain information could be 'classified' (this means it is restricted to certain people), or there could be sensitive issues that an organization does not consider appropriate for a supervisor to get involved in. So make sure you know where the 'No Trespassers' signs are!

At this stage of a project you are seeing how wide your investigation must range and how detailed it has to be.

However, face the fact that no one will spell out precisely from A to Z what you must do and how you will do it. (And if they did, you would lose out on the opportunity to use initiative and on the sense of achievement when it's all finished.)

## 3     Terms of reference

The subject and span of your project must now be expressed in words. The whole project will stem from this, so

make sure your terms of reference are clear and precise.

The phrase 'terms of reference' (shortened to TOR from now onwards) is to some people so familiar that they find it hard to put into other words. Yet to people who are starting their first project it is incomprehensible. Don't let it become a communication barrier.

TOR means *what you are to do.*

For instance, a job description could be called the TOR of one's employment. From another angle, TOR could be likened to a search warrant which allows the police to enter specified premises and search them.

Your project TOR authorize you to

> look into a ***certain matter***, within ***certain parameters***,
> for a ***specified purpose***.

So, you must set out, ***in writing***, what is to be undertaken.

## 3.1 Clear and precise

TOR must not be vague. 'To look into absenteeism' is far too sweeping. Whose absenteeism? ***Every*** employee, from part-time labourers to the Board of Directors?

And absenteeism over what period? Since the firm began in 1831?

No. TOR must be more definite than that. 'To analyse absenteeism in the prefabrication section during the last 12 months.'

This does tell us what the project is about. However, the TOR should also tell us the ***purpose*** of the project.

Let's look at some examples of Project TOR.

To examine the present system of induction for new employees, to identify shortcomings and make suggestions for improvements in the system.

To evaluate over the last three years the company's traditional Christmas gift of a turkey to each employee and to compare four alternatives that have been suggested by employees and make a recommendation.

Sometimes TOR are set out as short numbered statements of intent. This can make it even clearer just what is to be done and why.

**1.** To investigate Widget production hold-ups during the last 12 months due to component shortages.

**2.** To examine current procedures for replacing component stocks.

**3.** To devise a system for overcoming problems identified while carrying out 1 and 2.

You may be interested to read the TOR that were eventually written for Sam Sharp's project.

**1.** To examine the present production methods and layout in C, D and E workshops.

**2.** To assess the maximum production that could be achieved from present resources.

**3.** To make recommendations for any additional resources needed in order to achieve an increase of 50 per cent over production in the company's last financial year.

## 3.2 Agreeing the TOR

Your TOR are your authority to proceed, so the employer should agree the TOR of any work-based project. Indeed in bigger companies, where many people have undertaken projects in the past, the training manager may hand you a piece of paper headed 'Terms of Reference'. This is followed by a series of numbered paragraphs.

Great! – provided ***you*** are clear about what it is you have to do. (If not, why not try writing it down in your own words and then asking your immediate boss to check it out for you?)

Before you commence your project you should submit the TOR to your NEBSM course tutor who will confirm these with the assessor. This makes sure you are on the right tracks. Any observations from the tutor and the NEBSM assessor should be carefully noted because they are both very experienced people.

If you are stuck for ideas on what you might undertake for your project, have a look at Appendix B (Types of project).

## Activity 3

■ Time guide 10 minutes

Imagine that you are to undertake a project on 'Car Parking on Company Premises'. You have established that this means *all* vehicles using any of the designated car parking space (i.e. company vehicles and those of employees, visitors and VIPs).

You are expected to come up with ideas for alleviating present complaints: from visitors that they can find nowhere to park; from employees that there is haphazard parking which wastes space, is dangerous, blocks access, etc. You are also to look to future needs (a three-year span is suggested).

Try your hand at writing your TOR.

_____

_____

_____

_____

How did you get on? I didn't find it all that easy, maybe because I was trying the continuous form rather than short numbered statements of intent. This is what I came up with:

■ to investigate the present usage of parking space and to forecast the likely parking requirements for the next three years;

■ to make recommendations which will improve the present situation and cope with estimated needs for the next three years.

## 4     Planning

Having settled exactly what it is you are aiming to do, you need to be equally clear on *how*. Time spent on planning can save many wasted hours and much useless effort.

When you are ready to tackle the next stage, grab your rough pad and we'll start *planning*.

To begin with, you are looking at your project overall, to see *what is to be done*.

This is the point where some people's minds go totally blank, particularly when they have a project of the 'Is there a better way?' type.

A good starting point is the present situation – what happens *now*. Think of:

- sequence;
- people involved: where and how;
- space used;
- work flow;
- machines/equipment used;
- material/product/vehicles movement;
- etc., etc.

In other words, think of what happens now, but broken down into all its separate elements.

Having tuned your mind to your particular subject, pick up your pencil. Now, without bothering about the order, jot down all the things that occur to you in relation to your project. And leave a fair space between each item.

Note down the points as they come into your mind: don't worry that some are small matters and some are very important. One or two things you're jotting down now may even be scrubbed eventually: it doesn't matter.

Let your thoughts sweep across a broad range of aspects. Note each one down, but don't linger on anything; and, above all, don't start worrying about how and where and in what order.

What you are doing is a solo form of what the advertising world calls 'brainstorming'. One thought is triggering another. Look widely, making your mind use a wide-angled lens so that you view the whole panorama of the project. Grab each idea and quickly note it down but keep the thought momentum going.

Sit back and read the next Scene and then we'll practise brainstorming.

Helen Conway's office

**Case Study**

| *Players:* | *Helen Conway* <br> *Peter Conway* |
|---|---|
| *Helen:* | Come in, little brother. I'm sure this isn't just a social visit, so what's the problem? |
| *Peter:* | I'm in one hell of a fix, Helen, and you're the only person I can turn to. |
| *Helen:* | The new job hasn't fallen through, has it? I thought it was all signed and sealed. |
| *Peter:* | It is. Nothing wrong there. It's to do with the old firm actually. As you know, I leave in two months' time. |
| *Helen:* | To a brand-new house in Bristol, for which your new employers are providing a mortgage on very reasonable terms plus removal expenses. Right? |
| *Peter:* | Right. |
| *Helen:* | So what's the problem? |
| *Peter:* | It's the actual moving . . . you know, the home . . . Pam and me . . . to a new house 250 miles away. |
| *Helen:* | Good God, Peter! An electronics genius confessing he's unable to organize a mundane task like moving house. Don't let your new employers hear you – they might have second thoughts. |

| | |
|---|---|
| *Peter:* | Helen, shut up and listen! Of course I could organize the move if I were here, **but** I've got to go to Denmark. |
| *Helen:* | Denmark? How come? |
| *Peter:* | Remember that installation John Craybourne and I worked on? John was to go over and set it up and stay for the run-in period, probably about six weeks in all, working flat out. |
| *Helen:* | So? |
| *Peter:* | John's in hospital. Won't be back at work for at least two months. |
| *Helen:* | And you've agreed to go, leaving your pregnant wife with a load of worries she's in no condition to cope with. Honestly, Peter, if I were Pam I'd divorce you. |
| *Peter:* | What the blazes can I do? Apart from John, I'm the only one who can follow it through and keep the customer happy. I can't let the old firm down. |
| *Helen:* | What about joining the new job a few weeks later? |
| *Peter:* | No, they've a big project starting, in my field, so they need me fast. I've already pushed my starting date to the limit. |
| *Helen:* | What it is to be indispensable! So you've come to big sister for practical help – not for a shoulder to cry on? |
| *Peter:* | Yes. You're tops in organizing and managing... |
| *Helen:* | I also have a small but demanding business to manage... |
| *Peter:* | I know, but... well... if not for my sake, then for Pam's. She's not having an easy time with our first: she's got to be careful. |
| *Helen:* | Which is why I can't throw you out of my office! All right, let's get down to basics. You leave for Denmark when? |
| *Peter:* | Monday. |
| *Helen:* | And you'll get back how long before the removal men cometh? |
| *Peter:* | Maybe a week. I might make it earlier, but don't count on it. With a week at home I can do all the last-minute jobs. But I was looking to you to co-ordinate everything so that nothing gets overlooked. |
| *Helen:* | So, before Monday we shall have to go through what needs to be organized. |
| *Peter:* | I thought maybe we could do that on Saturday morning? |
| *Helen:* | Ouch! I was supposed to be... oh, well, I'll postpone that. OK, Peter, I'll come over on Saturday: and in the meantime I'll draw up a schedule of what needs to be done to get Pam and the home to Bristol without a miscarriage! |
| *Peter:* | Yes. We can sort out what can be left for me to do. And don't forget that Pam will want to be involved. |

| | |
|---|---|
| *Helen:* | Sure she will. I'm lumbered with the organization and the co-ordination. At least there's one mercy... |
| *Peter:* | What's that? |
| *Helen:* | You're moving out of a company house, so I'm not saddled with selling the old place. OK, Pete! Leave it with me. Big sister is at hand. |
| *Peter:* | Bless you Helen, I don't know how to thank you... |
| *Helen:* | Don't imagine I'm doing it for you: I'm thinking of the next generation of Conways! |

Blood ties would have to be pretty strong to take on such a task at the drop of a hat. Helen has got to do some imaginative thinking to produce a schedule for Saturday. Moving house involves so many things. Some major, some so small they can easily be overlooked. But those small things can make all the difference between a smooth operation and a frustrating one.

# Activity 4

■ Time guide 10 minutes

Imagine that it is *your* office and *your* brother who has dropped in with this removal problem. Have a brainstorming session. Get a large sheet of paper. Let your mind rove over the whole operation. What must your list include? Write down each point as it pops into your head. Write quickly so that the next thought isn't stifled. Don't worry about the order.

This is good practice for generating ideas. Make the imaginative part of your mind work for you as well as the practical side.

The list Helen came up with is in Appendix G. It's probable that her list is written a bit more personally than yours. But has she forgotten anything? Have you got anything vital on your list that she's missed? Has she put any items on her list that you haven't got?

**4.1
Planning a time
schedule**

When you are ready to press on, approach planning from a new angle. Consider *when*. Try to see what must be done within a time framework.

Always remember, *time flies*.

First you need to get some form of time-scale. You have already established certain time limits in settling your parameters: that's going to be a great help in preparing your schedule.

Start with the final submission date for the project report and work backwards from it.

Settle that and then make a rough chart, splitting up the *time* between *now* and *then* into convenient units. A week is probably the most practical, unless your investigation is very protracted, in which case you might start in months and then split, say, the last *three* months into weeks.

# Part B

A vertical chart makes it easier to write tasks in the appropriate week.

| Date | Week no. | Things to be done |
|---|---|---|
|  | 26 |  |
|  | 25 |  |
|  | 24 |  |
|  | 23 |  |

| Date | Week no. | Things to be done |
|---|---|---|
|  | 3 |  |
|  | 2 |  |
|  | 1 |  |
|  | Zero | Submit project report |

You'll put actual dates, of course, but it is a good idea to have the week numbered as well, working from the deadline backwards.

Having drafted your time chart roughly, rule it in ink on good quality paper or, better still, cardboard. The dates are fixed, so you can ink them in. The deadline is fixed, so, against the zero, ink in 'Submit project report'. Put anything else in pencil for the time being in case you want to reschedule it later on.

While you are drawing up your schedule, some time elements will probably spring into your mind: things that will have to be done at certain stages. If so, pencil them in.

Time flies fast.

**4.2 Time buffers**

In making out a time schedule, it is wise to leave gaps. Above all leave at least a week before your deadline. Thus, 'Project completed' will go into zero + 7 days. This is the final 'buffer'. But allow interim buffers for snags and unexpected delays. If you meet none, then you are so good that you're too good for this world!

**Project Danger Warning**

Lack of breathing space *can seriously damage your plan.*

You could ink in some more items towards the end of the schedule if you do a little time estimating. How long must you allow for the typing of the final copy of your project report? I would allow at least a week. That puts 'Typing of final report' at zero + 2 weeks, but build in a safety margin – make it zero + 3.

Your NEBSM tutor should read the final draft. (What's more, the tutor's eagle eye may spot an omission or anomaly that you were too involved to see.) Many calls are made on tutors' time, so you should allow two weeks. And if posting rather than personal delivery and collection is involved, it would be wise to allow another week for that.

Working further back, you will need time for the final editing and tidying up – at least another week. We're now at something like zero + 7 weeks and we've not written a word!

Time flies faster.

Will it take you a month to write up? Or, with a buffer for safety, 6 weeks? So, its zero + 13 for starting to write.

This means that all fact-finding has to be completed 3 months before the deadline.

Time flies faster than you think.

Are you beginning to realize how essential it is to have a time schedule? And to keep to it? Because, if you don't, you'll find...

Time has flown.

| Date | Week no. | Things to be done |
|------|----------|-------------------|
|      | 26       |                   |
|      | 25       |                   |
|      | 24       |                   |
|      | 23       |                   |

| Date | Week no. | Things to be done |
|------|----------|-------------------|
|      | 15       |                   |
|      | 14       | Complete investigation |
|      | 13       | Start writing draft report |
|      | 12       |                   |
|      | 11       |                   |
|      | 10       | Re-drafting       |
|      | 9        |                   |
|      | 8        | Clean up diagrams etc. |
|      | 7        | Final polish and edit |
|      | 6        | Submit to course tutor |
|      | 5        |                   |
|      | 4        |                   |
|      | 3        | Typing of final copy |
|      | 2        | Fair copies of charts & diagrams |
|      | 1        | Read through submission copy |
|      | Zero     | Submit project report |

**4.3**
**Planning in more detail**

Have you come across these lines by Kipling?

I have six honest serving men
They taught me all I knew
Their names are What and Why and When
And How and Where and Who.

*Why* and *What* and *When* have already been at work. Now you can use *How* and *Where* and *Who*.

Work from your brainstorming scribbles. Go through your rough list of what needs to be done. Consider each item and add notes for yourself on:

● *where* relevant information is or might be;

● *how* you can obtain it;

● *who* might be of help in locating it;

● *who* might be able to provide information.

At this stage you might like to glance at Appendix C (Ways of researching/where to research).

## 4.4
## Order of priority

While you are going through your list and thinking about what needs to be done you will be aware of varying degrees of urgency. (After all, the brainstorming you did was not tied to a particular order.) What about using symbols – letters, numbers, stars or coloured spots – to indicate priority? Award a priority 'value' to everything that is to be done.

At this detailed stage of planning you might realize that you may not have time to work on all the ideas you had. Some of those at the very bottom of the priority list may have to be ditched. In that case, allot a symbol for 'non-essentials'. Later on, it will remind you to do them, but only *if* you find that time has *not* flown.

## 4.5
## Working notes

Always rewrite any rough list that gets difficult to read. You want to reach a stage where you have clearly written sheets that you can work from.

If you have decided that index cards would suit your way of working, this is when you set them up.

Give a reference number to your sheets or cards, then you can make cross references where something on one sheet is related to, or even depends on, the outcome of another task.

Ultimately you should have a series of pages or cards, each with an idea on it, together with notes of:

● *what* you need to do;

● *where* you have to go;

● *who* must be approached;

● *priority* rating.

## 4.6
## Further items for the time schedule

By now you should be in a position to have another go at your time schedule.

Work from your lists and see where the various tasks could and should be slotted in. You will have to dovetail your work carefully. Decide which items can be conveniently overlapped.

(If your previous studies have included Critical Path Analysis, the time-planning of your project will be a practical application of the principles learned.)

If you need to write away for information, get the letters off as quickly as possible. It is always wise to allow plenty of time for replies to come in. There may be some work which hinges on the replies, but there will certainly be plenty of other jobs to get on with in the meantime.

In obtaining the co-operation and help of other people, allow for the possibility that they may not be available or may be away ill or on leave when you try to make contact. Also, they may have a time schedule of their own to work to, and *your* project may not be a number one priority for them!

In carrying out a project you cannot afford to leave things to the last moment. You must always make allowances for the unexpected. (Doesn't one of 'Murphy's Laws' state that if something *can't* happen, it will anyway!)

Your *time schedule* should stay at the work-base you prepared for yourself. Put it where you can see it, but not stuck to a wall. You will need to rub out some tasks and re-enter them in a different week. You will also be adding items. Your time schedule must always be 'get-at-able'.

*Susan White is a hairdresser who completed her apprenticeship in London before moving with her family to Penchester, a busy Midlands city. She now works for an established and successful family business. For the last two years she has been their number one in the salon.*

*She is go-ahead, lively and keen to progress, so the firm decided that it was time for her to have some supervisory management training. They sponsored her for a NEBSM course at the local college.*

*Susan is now involved in her project. The following details have been agreed between Susan herself, her employers and her NEBSM course tutor.*

*Title:* **The viability of a branch salon at Swanton**

*Terms of Reference:*

*1. To investigate the potential for a branch salon at Swanton.*

*2. To evaluate possible locations and assess the initial and running costs of suitable premises.*

*3. To assess and cost out the equipment and staffing required.*

*4. To make recommendations.*

*Sue was excited at the thought of this project and the possibilities within it for herself – she might become manageress. But she decided that hopes of promotion (career development, really) must not colour the investigations or bias her subsequent recommendations.*

*She decided to treat the project as if it were her own money that would be invested (not that she had any money, of course, but she could pretend an imaginary Uncle Silas had left her a legacy).*

*She carried out a brainstorming session, putting each idea on to a separate index card. She added fresh cards as additional thoughts occurred during the next few days: there was quite a pile of cards now.*

*About a week later she decided she had too many cards. It was difficult to juggle all the ideas. With some effort she managed to group together some of the single ideas under one heading. She then made out new cards for the headings, inserting additional comments as she went along.*

*She was surprised how well this worked. The original number of cards had been reduced to a third and the file box was tidy and manageable. What was more, her own mind was tidy, having a clearer idea of what had to be done.*

*Sue's revised card file is set out on the next page. It is not in any particular order but it demonstrates that here brainstorming had covered a wide area.*

*While rewriting her cards she had noted possible **who**'s and **where**'s for gathering information. No doubt she would eventually realize that there would not be enough time to undertake all the areas of investigation she had thought of, but she set herself high standards, and that's no bad thing.*

# Activity 5

■ Time guide 20 minutes

Consider Sue's cards. Give a priority rating (including noting those things that may have to be omitted). Now plan a time schedule on the blank form. Swanton is a market town some 15 km from Penchester. The firm will allow her time off and pay expenses to carry out investigations there on four separate days. Assume there are 26 weeks to *Deadline*.

---

**PREMISES.**
"LOCK-UP TYPE"

GOOD LOCATION NEAR TOWN CENTRE (AVOID HIGH COST PRECINCT)
CHECK LOCAL ESTATE AGENTS

NEED NOT BE AN EXISTING HAIRDRESSING SALON

---

**PREMISES**
POSSIBLE PURCHASE
WITH A FLAT ABOVE? (s/c)
(INCOME FROM LETTING USEFUL)
SEE - ESTATE AGENTS. LOCAL PRESS
CHECK RECENT OLD ADS FOR INFO
FLAT? ME FIRST REFUSAL !!!   N.b. BE OBJECTIVE SUE

---

**PLANNING.**
CHANGE OF USE? ANY SNAGS?
SEE TOWN PLANNING DEPT — TALK OVER PROBLEM.

HOW TO MAKE AN APPLICATION.
WHAT COST INVOLVED?

---

**DECORATIONS**
(SHOP INTERIOR)

FIND SMALL DECORATOR WHO KNOWS HIS JOB.
PLUS — SIGN WRITER.
HOW TO WORK OUT A COST?
*All Guesstimates* !!!

---

**FIXTURES & FITTINGS**
BASINS - PLUMBING - POWER SKTS
LIGHTING ETC. ETC. ETC.
(FOR BUILDERS SEE SHOP FIT LIST)
PLUS — HANDY ELECTRICIAN
FRIENDLY PLUMBER.
GUESSTIMATING LIKE MAD.

---

**OVERHEADS** GENERAL?
RENT [IF A LOCK-UP]?
RATES - WATER - PHONE
ELECTRICITY — (CHECK OLD SHOP ACCOUNTS FOR FIGURES)
WOULD A CHANGE OF USE MEAN RE- RATING PREMISES? LIKELY INCREASE
CHECK WITH RATING OFFICER

---

**COMPETITION ???**
CHECK OUT TOWN CENTRE
HOW MANY? CHECK THEIR PRESENTATION STANDARDS - CLEANLINESS. HOURS/DAYS OPEN
TYPE OF CLIENTELE? PRICES?
GAPS IN SERVICE OFFERED? BE DISCREET !!!

---

**FLAT ABOVE SHOP?**
IF LET - HOW?
FURNISHED? — UNFURNISHED?
GOING RATE IN TOWN?
CHECK LOCAL RAG.
ANY LEGAL SNAGS?
CHECK OUT WITH COLLEGE LAW LECTURER (a Dishy number Jim)

---

**— ADVERTISING —**
CHECK WITH LOCAL WEEKLY RAG
COST OF ADVERTISING.
BIG SPLASH FOR OPENING DAY
REGULAR SPOTS.
*Don't tell them who you are* YET.

---

**SHOP STOCK**
BASIC STOCK FOR SALON.
PLUS FOR RESALE TO CUSTOMERS
LIST PENCHESTER SHOP STOCK
COULD WE IMPROVE ON THIS?
CHECK TRADE JOURNALS FOR IDEAS AND COSTS — SEE REF LIBRARY

---

**NOTE TO SELF**
WEEKS 14 & 15
SUNNING IT IN GREECE
BygThen I'll need sleep more than sun ?????

---

**FUTURE POTENTIAL**
IS THE TOWN STILL GROWING?
CHECK REF. LIBRARY
FOR POPULATION BREAKDOWN
TOWN + 5 MILE AREA
ASK AT LOCAL PRESS ??

---

**? → SUSAN WHITE ← ?**

YOU ARE A NATURALLY DISORGANISED ANIMAL ...
HAVE YOU THOUGHT THROUGH ALL THE ESSENTIALS ???

---

**SHOP FITTING**
(EXTERIOR)
IF CHANGE OF USE - COST OF REFIT?
IF EXISTING - COST OF REFIT?
CHECK 3 LOCAL BUILDERS
1 LARGE - 1 SMALL OUTFIT AND TWO MEN & A DOG SET UP.
NO QUOTES - JUST GUESSTIMATES

---

**STAFF**
LOCAL WAGES AS PENCHESTER?
PART TIMERS AVAILABLE?
TRAINEES?
[GOVERNMENT SCHEMES FOR 16 TO 18s — AND OTHERS]
CHECK WITH—
LOCAL JOBS CENTRE

---

**EQUIPMENT**
MAKE A LIST OF ALL EQUIPMENT NEEDED TO START —
DRYERS - MIRRORS - CHAIRS - TOWELS - OVERALLS ETC.
MAKE LIST OF PENCHESTER EQUIPMENT ONE EVENING.
? SECOND HAND BARGAINS IN TRADE PRESS

---

**A MARKET SURVEY**
BY S. WHITE & CO.
TAKE A DAY OFF (MARKET DAY?)
ASK WOMEN IF/WHERE THEY HAVE HAIR DONE. WHY?
ARE THEY SATISFIED?
WOULD THEY LIKE SOMETHING EXTRA?
WHAT?? (I'D BE SCARED STIFF) COULD BE FUN

---

**REPORT PREP NOTES**
ALLOW 2 WEEKS FOR TUTOR TO CHECK OVER *BEFORE* FINAL TYPING
ALLOW 1 WEEK TO AMEND AND REWRITE. (HOPE NOT)
MUM WILL TYPE FINAL IN THE EVENINGS: KNOWING MUM ALLOW 3 WEEKS AT LEAST

| Date | Week no. | Things to be done |
|---|---|---|
|  |  |  |
|  |  |  |
|  |  |  |
|  |  |  |
|  |  |  |
|  |  |  |
|  |  |  |
|  |  |  |
|  |  |  |
|  |  |  |
|  |  |  |
|  |  |  |
|  |  |  |
|  |  |  |
|  |  |  |
|  |  |  |
|  |  |  |
|  |  |  |
|  |  |  |
|  |  |  |
|  |  |  |
|  |  |  |
|  |  |  |
|  |  |  |
|  |  |  |
|  |  |  |

## 5      Summary

- Have you prepared a work-base for yourself?
- Have you collected together the 'tools' that you need?
- Are you quite sure what your project is?
- Do you know how widely you are to investigate?
- Do you clearly understand what you have to do?
- Are your TOR set down clearly?

- Have the TOR been agreed with:

  - your employer (for a work-based project) or the 'validator' (for other types of project);

  - your course tutor and the NEBSM assessor?

- Have you had your ideas session (brainstorming)?

- Have you made out your time schedule?

- Have you made out lists or cards of 'Jobs to be done'?

- Do you know what tasks *you* are to do?

- Do you know when you are going to do them?

- Are you organized and *ready to start your project?*

This is the end of the 'sitting and thinking about it' stage. You can unwrap the wet towel that has been around your head.

Now you put on your armour, for deflecting any mild rebuffs,
your charm, for eliciting information,
your smile, for gaining co-operation,

*and you get it all together.*

## 1     The facts of the matter

You may be undertaking something that you feel strongly about. From the motivation angle this is splendid.

However, don't let your enthusiasm take the form of missionary zeal to convert people to your point of view. Rather be a Sherlock Holmes who patiently probes, seeking out the truth of the matter.

The basis of your work must be *facts*. This means *what actually was* – not what you think it might or should have been – and *what is* – not what you'd prefer it to be or imagine it probably is.

In carrying out your project, you must put aside your personal feelings. To do this, take 'the fly on the wall' approach. Look at the situation as if it had nothing to do with you. Although you have inside knowledge, remain *outside* the situation. Above all, *shut your prejudices out*.

A works canteen

**Case Study**

| | |
|---|---|
| *Players*: | *Sid Beals, Supervisor* |
| | *Fred Dykes, Supervisor* |

*(Sid and Fred sitting at a table with cups of tea)*

| | |
|---|---|
| *Fred:* | So you think these robots you've been looking into aren't much cop? |
| *Sid:* | Too right, mate. When I knew my project was to investigate robotics for the precision-winding shop, I knew what I'd find. Bloody computers – can't even get our wages right. Our work is highly skilled: it's skilled men that are essential, not electronic toys. |
| *Fred:* | You're right. You and me have been skilled craftsmen for years. Bloody computers can't teach us anything: we could lose them. |
| *Sid:* | Exactly. You should have seen the place in Germany that's got them. A load of blokes in white coats dashing about while machine minders looked on – not a skilled man among them. |
| *Fred:* | No skilled men in precision-winding? They must be mad. |
| *Sid:* | You're right there, Fred. We don't need to worry about competition from that lot. It was a shambles. Must cost a fortune in white coats, let alone the bods in them. |
| *Fred:* | So you reckon robots are not for us? Then what will you recommend? |
| *Sid:* | Stay as we are. If craft work goes and computers take over, we'll go out of business. |
| *Fred:* | Good for you Sid. We need a bloke like you to stop whiz-kids rocking the boat. |

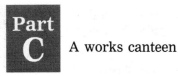

**Case Study**

Let's try this study again, but with two different players.

*Players*:  *Dave Keen, Supervisor*
*Bill Cobb, Supervisor*

*(Dave and Bill sitting at a table with cups of tea)*

*Bill:* But, Dave, you used to say nothing could replace the kind of skills needed in precision-winding. Craft work is craft work.

*Dave:* I know I did, Bill, but this project of mine has really opened my eyes. I've actually seen robots working and they can go on doing it 24 hours a day, seven days a week.

*Bill:* You're pulling my leg. Machines break down – and I bet your robots do.

*Dave:* Sure, but I checked out that six trained mechanics were all that was needed to keep 80 machines going. What's more, I never counted more than eight out of action at any one time – and that included maintenance.

*Bill:* We could work a three-shift system here if we had the orders.

*Dave:* And why haven't we got the orders?

*Bill:* You tell me.

*Dave:* Costs, that's what. My project isn't just about looking at alternative machines, but taking a hard look at the figures. The facts are bone-shaking. The reject rate from those robots doing miniature matrix-coiling is down from our 9 per cent to under 1 per cent. And break-down time only adds 1 per cent to costs.

*Bill:* I can't believe it.

*Dave:* I can see real possibilities for robots in bays C and D.

*Bill:* I never thought I'd hear you talk like that, Dave. A lifetime of craft and skill thrown out of the window – that's what you're suggesting.

*Dave:* No, Bill, the way my project is shaping shows that a lot of our really skilled men are wasted on semi-skilled work.

*Bill:* True. Much of my day is wasted.

*Dave:* I reckon we must improve quality, cut waste, and spend time on designing new equipment. Skills are needed there.

*Bill:* Hope for some of us them?

*Dave:* Hope lies in getting costs down to a market price! You know, Bill, there's so much I hadn't realized. You can spend half a lifetime working in your own specialized patch and not see what's happening outside. You need to take a break – stand outside and take a fresh look.

*Bill:* Do a project, you mean?

*Dave:* Perhaps. If I hadn't had to do mine. I'd still be thinking in the same old way and the rest of the world could have passed by me and I wouldn't have known.

In these two short scenes the relative merits or demerits of robotics is irrelevant. What is relevant is the difference in attitudes between Sid and Dave and their approach to their projects.

Sid is obviously a craftsman in a specialized trade. He has fixed views on anything that may affect his status. Thus he sets out on this fact-finding already convinced of the final outcome. He sees only what he wants to see. He collects only the evidence that will support his preconceived notions. Anything that does not fit into his set ideas is discarded.

Dave, on the other hand, makes an honest endeavour to discount preconceptions. The facts begin to speak for themselves. The accumulation of evidence opens his mind. Ideas sprout. This is how it should be.

**Project
Danger
Warning**

A closed mind
*can seriously stifle new ideas.*

| 2 | Gathering and gleaning |
|---|---|

You are now right at the heart of the project: you are *doing* what you set out to do. Accept that it may be a long process. It takes time to collect information, to experiment, to do a worthwhile project. Be patient, maintain a sense of purpose.

Remember that you will need supporting evidence for any statements you make in your report. For example, it is no use saying:

'Although up to about three years ago Fizzit was the most popular brand, it has now been overtaken by Whizzit, and even Tizzit sells more.'

This is such a loose statement that it means almost nothing. If the three items are being compared, we need to know how much 'more popular' Fizzit was and Whizzit is. And if Tizzit is a relevant part of the picture, where did it stand three years ago against the other two and where does it stand today?

The statement cries out for quantitative data to support it.

In fact, this sort of data can be very effectively put into graphic form. In Appendix D there is a bar chart which compares three items. Take a look at it and see how it would support the broad statement about Fizzit, Whizzit and Tizzit.

## Activity 6

■ Time guide 10 minutes

You are reading through the draft of a friend's project report. This is concerned with productivity. You have just read the following:

'Production has dropped because of shorter product runs.'

Note down what sort of facts and figures your friend needs to back up his statement.

_____

_____

_____

_____

The sort of data I feel he should seek is *actual* product runs in a previous period and in the period under review. He then needs to work out for each period the average length of runs and, if setting-up time is relevant, the number of product changes.

One thing he should definitely state is *how much* production has dropped. After all, one pin less in a pin-making factory is actually a drop in production! And unless one pin is going to be like the horse-shoe nail that lost a kingdom, that sort of drop is irrelevant!

Where you need to get opinions or reactions, tread warily and do not let your attitudes affect your objectivity. Nor should you let those with loud mouths influence your judgement.

You should quantify. To say 'a majority were in favour of this change' could be misleading. If there was a total of 21 people, 11 are a majority. Ten people strongly opposed to the 'change' could mean difficult times ahead! So avoid imprecise statements and quote actual figures or percentages.

Never think that questionnaires are an easy option. If you want to use a questionnaire and you have no previous experience of preparing one, seek advice from someone who knows the pitfalls. At least, make yourself aware of how *not* to word questions.

## Activity 7

■ Time guide 3 minutes

Canteen views

Read the three questions below and mark against each whether you think it is 'S' (suitable) or 'U' (unsuitable) for a questionnaire that all personnel are being asked to complete. While you are doing this, try to think what makes the question suitable or unsuitable.

1 Do you use the canteen? 

| Yes | No |

2 What meals do you prefer? 

| Yes | No |

3 Do you think there should be reserved tables for different grades of personnel? 

| Yes | No |

The first question is not suitable because it is like those other loose statements we've been looking at. It tells the person who is investigating very little.

Those saying 'yes' to this question could include daily users of the canteen and someone who happened to use it once when he'd left his 'snap box' on the bus? The investigator would need to differentiate between regular and occasional users.

Question 2 would make the collating of the answers very difficult. As it stands, I suspect there would be a few jokers who would delight in putting specialities of other countries, such as birds' nests, frogs' legs, sheep's eyes!

Question 3 could be suitable, but would probably need to be followed by other questions to get something more specific from those answering 'yes'.

Basic books on statistics usually include a section on questionnaires.

---

## 3  Sorting and sifting

Gathering your information together is rather like a jigsaw puzzle, but one where there is no picture on the lid of the box! Some bits obviously relate to one another, others seem quite irrelevant. But at this stage nothing should be rejected.

When you sift through information try to keep like with like. Oddments can be clipped together and put on one side. If any item subsequently becomes significant, you know where to find it.

**3.1
Keeping a wide
vision**

A project is good management training. It makes you look at the whole picture so that you see things from a wider viewpoint than the usual work routine allows.

Beware of the dangers of the 'busy bee syndrome' to which many of us succumb. We put our conscience to sleep by buzzing happily on a straightforward task, which expands and expands. Meanwhile sleeping conscience ignores knotty matters. As time passes those knots get knottier.

Do not absorb yourself in one aspect that is comparatively easy to tackle and ignore the overall picture.

**Project
Danger
Warning**

The busy bee syndrome
*can endanger essentials.*

So, how are you progressing?

You made out a plan and a time schedule: refer to them, and keep on referring to them. But, bear in mind that a plan is *only* a plan – an intention. It is an aid that *you* have prepared to help you monitor your progress.

Don't let your plan become a strait-jacket that will impair movement. After all, it may be necessary to change priorities. Your plan should be flexible, not something that is carved in tablets of stone.

**Project
Danger
Warning**

An inflexible plan:
*the gaoler of opportunity.*

Any building contractor knows that, however detailed the specification, as the work progresses there will be variations and extras. These are necessary if the desired outcome is to be achieved.

You too will make variations and find extras that have to be undertaken. Useful evidence can arise quite unexpectedly. A chance remark in the daily work routine can lead you to an entirely new information source. Also, as the work on your project proceeds, you may find additional aspects that need to be looked into.

It is then you will be thankful for the time buffers you put in when planning your schedule?

**3.2
Using your data**

Once you have accumulated all your facts it will be necessary to analyse them. What is their significance? What light do they shed on the problem you are investigating?

In the next section we'll look at ways of analysing data.

## 4      Analyzing the data

It is impossible to lay down hard-and-fast rules for analysing data. The type of data collected will vary with the particular project undertaken. The way in which the facts are analysed and assessed will vary with the type of information collected.

**4.1
What to seek**

In looking at data you may be seeking:

- significance (importance);

- insignificance (not worth bothering about);

- similarities in pattern that can tell a tale;

- differences in pattern that also tell a tale;

- anomalies that 'don't quite add up';

- danger signals;

- patterns that suggest trends, giving a glimpse of the future.

In nearly every case it is easier to comprehend data if the facts are set out in a visual form.

Many cartoonists have latched on to the usefulness of a graph for making a wry comment on a situation.

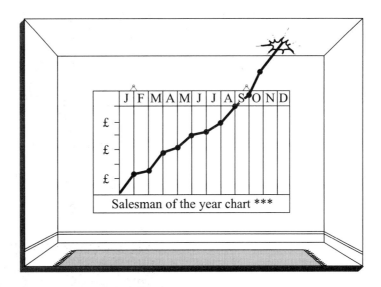

**4.3**
**Thinking on paper**

Try out some **rough** visual representations of data. Squared paper can be very handy for this. It provides a basic scale without the need for rulers and a lot of calculation. More accurate visuals can be drawn up later if required.

Graphs and bar charts are useful aids to seeing what lies behind data which are concerned with **how many** and **how much**. For instance:

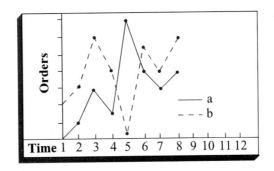

You can plot one item on a graph and be surprised when another item is plotted.

(Here you would be seeking the reason for the big difference in period 5.)

If we only see figures without plotting them on a graph we may not be aware of certain patterns.

For instance, on this graph the solid line follows a similar pattern to the dotted line, but it is one period later and this could be of considerable significance.

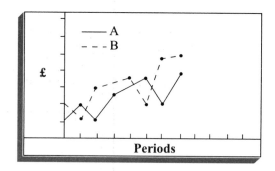

You might be seeking to adjust an imbalance, say over-manning or under-manning. This next example makes it obvious when serving and kitchen staff are most needed.

| | |
|---|---|
| Mon | |
| Tues | |
| Wed | |
| Thur | |
| Fri | |
| Sat | |
| Sun | |

Average number of meals served daily

Nowadays there are many examples of graphs and charts in newspapers and journals. Even where the particular article is not of interest to you, it is worth noting which type of visual is being used and the sort of data it is representing.

| Make | Features ratings | | | | |
|---|---|---|---|---|---|
| | a | b | c | d | e |
| A | ••• | •• | • | •••• | ••• |
| B | • | ••• | ••••• | ••• | •• |
| C | •• | • | ••• | ••• | ••• |
| D | ••••• | •• | • | •• | •• |
| E | ••• | ••••• | •• | • | •••• |

Features

a

b

c

d

e

By using what is called a 'matrix' the magazine *Which?* compares the relative merits of different makes of equipment/machines. Usually a note says 'the more spots the better'.

There are also some excellent visuals in the way of charts and graphs to be seen on the television screen in news and documentary programmes.

It is a matter of finding the appropriate visual for your facts: one that will show the real picture behind the data.

**4.4 Thinking in terms of space**

If you are considering space or area, it is better to have a precise scale. Space is something that most minds are bad at visualizing accurately, so use a ground plan that is to scale.

When dealing with layout, mark entrances, exits, passageways, windows. Then making cutout pieces (also to scale) for objects that occupy the space. Move the cut-outs around. Experiment to find the best layout.

**4.5 Maps**

You could be looking at blanks or 'thin' patches. These might be an indication of something needing attention, or they could be areas for development.

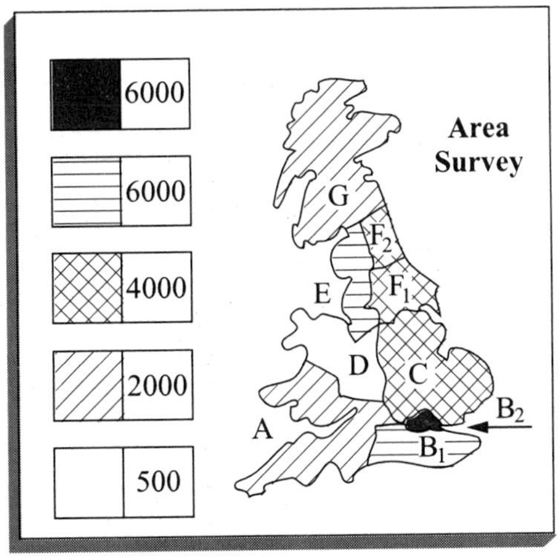


It should not be necessary to draw a map more than once. Prepare an outline and use a copier to obtain a number of copies. You can experiment with ways of filling in information and then transfer the chosen form to your final copy when required.

**Part C**

To sum up: in analyzing data we are seeking the reality that lies behind the statistics. We are looking for clues, for the footprints that will lead us to a new viewpoint, something that will enable us to see the situation more clearly.

Folklore exists in many organizations, often exaggerated over the years. Don't let it delude you and lead you to ill-considered notions.

Above all, illusions must not mask what *is* or what *was*.

**Project
Danger
Warning**

A desert mirage
*is but sand in the eye.*

'A taverner's tale'

**Case
Study**

*Philip Martin is the landlord of your local, a small friendly establishment. In conversation he discovers that you are doing a NEBSM training course, working away at your project. He is impressed.*

*'Lucky you,' says Phil ruefully. 'I could do with some training'.*

*'What for?' you enquire. 'This is a good pub – always busy.'*

*'You're right there,' says Phil. 'I've had to get in extra bar help to cope – not that the increased business seems to be doing me much good.'*

*'How's that?' you ask.*

*'I don't exactly know – that's the problem. All I know is my bank balance doesn't seem as good as it should be.'*

*'You'll have to take a hard look at the figures,' you suggest.*

*Phil makes a little grimace and says, 'I'm no good with figures. Pay into the bank, pay the bills and leave the rest to my accountant – that's me.' The he shakes his head and continues: 'But I've got a nasty feeling that something's not right, know what I mean?'*

*'Well, you're a jolly good landlord,' you reply.*

*'Not if I'm losing money, I'm not!'*

*To resolve this sad tavern tale, you agree to see if you can spot something wrong with Phil's figures.*

*'With all your study, you should be able to sort me out,' says Phil.*

*You are not so sure!*

*Phil gives you a note of his gross monthly taking that he banked in the last nine months, together with a list of his total purchases for the same period. You learn that there has been no change in prices and his stock stays pretty constant.*

Phil's list:

| Purchases | Month 1 – £4,500 | Month 2 – £5,000 | Month 3 – £6,000 |
| | Month 4 – £7,000 | Month 5 – £7,000 | Month 6 – £7,000 |
| | Month 7 – £8,000 | Month 8 – £8,000 | Month 9 – £8,000 |
| Takings | Month 1 – £5,850 | Month 2 – £6,500 | Month 3 – £7,800 |
| | Month 4 – £9,100 | Month 5 – £9,100 | Month 6 – £9,000 |
| | Month 7 – £10,200 | Month 8 – £10,100 | Month 9 – £10,000 |

You may be like Phil, not a 'figures' person. Don't worry, you will learn as you go. On the other hand, if you are mathematically bright, just remember that Phil isn't and a graph may show Phil what the figures mean.

## Activity 8

■ Time guide 15 minutes

With the figures provided, prepare a graph to show the purchases and takings over the nine-month period. Use squared or graph paper; give yourself plenty of space to make it easy to plot the figures.

When you have finished, look and see if the graph tells you a story.

Having thought about it, turn to Appendix H and see how the graph there compares with yours. You'll also find some comments about this case.

| 5 | **Having ideas on answers/solutions/improvements** |

In looking objectively at the fact of the matter – in analysing, mixing, matching, comparing – you have been using that part of your brain that does logical thinking.

It is time to consider all the courses of action that could possibly be implemented. This is where you need fresh ideas or new angles on old ideas. You use the imaginative part of your brain.

You need to relax and let your thoughts move across and through and around this situation you have investigated. Is there another way of looking at it? Turn it upside down, inside out, be inventive. Use 'ideas' like stepping-stones.

Don't reject any possibility at this stage, even if it has disadvantages that seem to loom large. Lurking within that possibility there could be the seed of another idea. That seed may germinate into a viable and realistic solution.

If your mind doesn't seem to be coming up with very much, here is something that might get the ideas generator going.

During your investigation you have probably become aware of what caused the situation to get to the stage of needing attention. By considering each root cause, one at a time, you may stimulate ideas on improvements or solutions.

Do not despair if inspiration does not come at once. Sleep on it: let your subconscious mind work for you.

Eventually you will get to the stage where pen and paper (or cards) are needed. Set out, on separate sheets,

1. what options there are;

2. changes that could be made.

## 6        Evaluating your options

A careful evaluation must now be made of each of the options.

To avoid blurring the issues, take three separate steps in evaluating.

1. *Weigh up the costs.*

2. *Weigh up the benefits.*

3. *Assess the effects.*

Let's look at each step in turn and see what it involves.

### 6.1
### Weighing up
### the costs

Everything has a cost. It may be possible to express that cost in terms of pounds and pence (i.e. *how much*). But there are also costs in terms of other resources (i.e. *who* and *what* is involved).

Look at the full resource cost of each option you have written down. To help you do this, here are some questions to answer.

- Is there a cash outlay? How much?

- What is the manpower cost: (a) in time; (b) in effort?

- Would there be additional usage of machines/equipment/materials/space/vehicles?

- If any option includes building alterations, what inconvenience cost might there be?

Checking out the costs of the options may become a mini-project in itself. But it has to be done. You want to make a complete job of this project, so there is no room for casual assumptions.

Whatever recommendations you finally make must be solidly based on a *full-facts* foundation!

# Activity 9

■ Time guide 15 minutes

'Never Cook the Facts'

(*Note*: The facts and figures in this case study are fictional. They are not based on any make or model currently available for purchase.)

Imagine that two of your friends, Harry and Sybil, together with their two daughters Penny and Patsy (aged 12 and 13), are moving into a 20-year old house they have just bought. It is in good decorative order, but the cooker in the kitchen is ancient and will have to be replaced. You decide to carry out a mini-project for them.

Your investigation reveals that there are three possible electric cookers (models A, B and C) and similar cooking facilities are provided by three gas cookers (models D, E and F).

You also look at microwave ovens. Their facilities cannot be equated, but Penny and Patsy asked you to include them.

Facts you discover:

1  Electricity company advises that the wiring from fuse-board to cooker supply box needs replacing for safety reasons. Cost £60.

2  Gas company advises that there would be no connection charge for a gas cooker becase a sealed-off connection pipe already exists in the kitchen.

3  Running costs of gas cookers seem be be about 10 per cent cheaper than electric cookers.

4  The old cooker has a part-exchange value if an electric cooker is purchased. The PX value depends on which model is purchased.

5  Prices and PX:

| Type | Model | Price | Model | Price | Model | Price |
|------|-------|-------|-------|-------|-------|-------|
| Electric | A | £320 | B | £380 | C | £450 |
| PX if buying | A | £10 | B | £20 | C | £50 |
| | | | | | (Special offer) | |
| Gas | D | £300 | E | £370 | F | £420 |
| Microwave | G | £150 | H | £200 | J | £250 |

*Action*

Get a rough pad and set out the cost facts in a form that you could include in your report. Make a note of the recommendations that would be made if based only on weighing the cash outlay costs.

We will take this mini-project a stage further after reading 'weighing up the benefits', so hang on to what you have just done.

**6.2
Weighing up the benefits**

Having assessed the cost of each option, consider the benefits.

Some benefits can be expressed in money terms:

● greater turnover;

● less expense outlay.

Some may be in terms of savings:

● improved use of resources;

● better use of time.

Others could be factors such as:

● greater safety;

● healthier working conditions;

● better design;

● better facilities;

● and so on. . . .

## Activity 10

■ Time guide 15 minutes

'Never Cook the Facts'

Get out your table of costs. Did you find that from a cash outlay point of view a gas cooker would seem to win hands down whichever grade of model is chosen? But probably you were also saying to yourself that it would be unwise to make a decision without taking other facts into consideration. So, to continue with the mini-project.

As well as prices, you obtained the following information:

Model A:   Good design, standard oven, four hobs, timer switch, small eye-level grill, plate-warming cabinet, choice of two colours.

Model B:   Luxury finish, large oven with glass door, four hobs, clock/timer control, eye-level grill, plate-warming cabinet, choice of three colours.

Model C:   Ultra-modern design, large oven, glass door, self-clean, rotisserie, lower simmer-oven, four ceramic hobs, electronic controls, clock, eye-level grill, choice of five colours.

Model D:   Basic model, small oven, four hobs, clockwork oven timer, grill under hobs, available in cream/white.

Model E:   Standard model, large oven with autolight, four autolight hobs, clock/timer on batteries, eye-level grill, plate-warming cabinet, choice of four colours and white.

Model F:   Luxury model, large oven with glass door and removable walls, four autolight hobs, electronic timer controls, eye-level grill, plate-warming cabinet, choice of three colours.

Model G:   Basic model, two heat setting (defrost and high), oven 0.6 cu. ft, heat power 500 watts.

Model H:   Medium-range model, four heat settings, oven 0.9 cu. ft, turntable, heat power 650 watts.

Model J:   Quality-range model, heat controls variable with push button, oven 1.1 cu. ft, turntable + stirrer, heat power 700 watts.

Now spend a little time thinking about the relative benefits that must be made clear to your friends. Take into consideration the fact that both Sybil and Harry have full-time jobs.

Again, jot down your ideas, and then read on ('assessing the effects').

_____

_____

_____

_____

_____

_____

**6.3**
**Assessing the effects**

This is also a weighing-up process, and a very important one. You now concentrate on seeing what effects each option would have on

*the organization itself*, and
*the people within that organization.*

Some effects are obvious. For instance, an option to buy a machine that will do five people's work, in effect makes five people redundant. This is a factor in any decision to buy the machine. A report that recommends the purchase of the machine must therefore comment on this factor.

There are effects that are difficult to measure or assess: an improved working environment; pleasanter surrounding; people's attitudes; better human relations; better public relations. Such things are difficult to evaluate, but must be considered.

You should endeavour to see all the effects, both bad and good.

It may be possible to circumvent or minimize 'bad' effects, and this you should consider. For instance, where 'change' is envisaged, can the ground be prepared beforehand? It is far better to have consultation before the change than confrontation after it.

# Activity 11

---

■ Time guide 15 minutes

'Never Cook the Facts'

Let's return to the case study.

When you weighed up the benefits, did you find that the electric models began to come into consideration? There seemed to be a number of features that could be attractive to people who are out all day at work: the cookers are clean and safe and have good timing devices for leaving prepared food to cook itself by a certain time.

A point which may not have struck you is that although the rewiring of the electric supply is a cost, the updated wiring is a benefit.

In the report to your friends, it might be best to set the benefits out in the form of a matrix: certainly this would show the various features that the suppliers emphasize.

Now tackle the third stage of this mini-project. Here are some further facts for your consideration:

1  Sybil prefers cooking with gas: she finds it easier to control the heating. She learned to cook on gas, her mother used it and she had it in the house they are leaving. She is a traditionalist.

2  Harry is easy either way, except that he says he's not made of money. He's an appreciative eater but not keen on cooking, which, with three women in the house, he hopes to avoid.

3  Penny and Patsy are highly nervous of gas and never use it if Mum or Dad are not around. That's why they asked you to look at microwaves, which some of their school friends rave about.

*continued overleaf*

---

Try to make some assessment now of the effects on the family and on the individuals. Then read the next section on 'Coming to conclusions'.

_____

_____

_____

_____

_____

_____

## 7      Coming to conclusions

You set out the options on separate cards or sheets. For each option you noted the costs and benefits. You have also noted the effects on the organization and the people within it.

Now you can look at each option in turn and consider its advantages and disadvantages. This gives you the basis for comparison and for coming to conclusions. For instance:

Option A is preferable to Option B;

Option C would work provided that...

Option D could be adopted now.

Such and such events would have to transpire before Option E could be adopted.

You might even come to the conclusion that none of the options is better than the situation as it stands at present.

Having reached conclusions by this careful weighing-up process, you should know what **_recommendations_** you will be making.

Let's take a final look at our mini-project. I am sure you will agree that the matter was not as straightforward as it appeared at first.

Cost alone seemed to favour gas. Benefits seemed to favour electric cookers. When the human aspects came into it an entirely new set of factors emerged. Maybe in presenting your findings to the family you might even have recommended that they consider the option of buying a cheaper gas or electric model _and_ a microwave. The final decision would, of course, have been theirs.

**Project
Danger
Warning**

Grabbing first options
_can fog best solutions._

- Have you collected all the facts you need?
- Have you researched sufficiently? That is to say:
  - have you covered an adequate period and/or
  - have you looked into enough alternatives?
- Have you analysed the data?
- Have you experimented with graphic forms for your data?
- Have you got everything possible *from* your data?
- Have you relegated rubbish and red herrings to the waste bin?
- Have you considered all possible options?
- Have you fully evaluated your options by:
  - weighing the costs?
  - weighing the benefits?
  - assessing the effects?
- Have you reached logical conclusions?
- Do you know what your recommendations are going to be?
- Have you considered *all* the implications of your recommendations?
- Have you carried out your TOR?

While you have been undertaking a project you have been concentrating on:

- *doing*

    – in collecting evidence;

- *thinking*

    – in analysing evidence;

- *creative thinking*

    – in searching for solutions;

- *logical thinking*

    – in coming to conclusions;

- *decision making*

    – in shaping recommendations.

All of this was being done by *you* for *your* project.

Now you have to *share* your experience with others by means of words on paper.

You are at the end of a long journey. Now you must think back to the beginning. The readers of your report have to be told:

- what you set out to do;

- what you did;

- the conclusions you came to;

- your recommendations;

- what they will cost.

## 1. Style

We all speak in a different way on different occasions, for example:

- in applying for a job;

- in chatting at the sports club;

- in visiting Great Aunt Agatha;

- in playing with the kids.

Similarly, we write in a different style and we may even use quite different sorts of words for:

(a) a *holiday postcard* to colleagues;

(b) a *memo* to another department;

(c) a *letter* to a customer apologizing for a delay in delivery;

(d) a *report*, such as you are now concerned with.

# Activity 12

■ Time guide 3 minutes

Here are some sentences in different styles. Match them to the different forms of written communication above by putting (a), (b), (c) or (d) after each one.

1 In the despatch department, orders stamped *today* in red are given priority. _____

2 Re. X and Co. Customer irate over delay. Please check with shippers and give me chapter and verse. _____

3 We regret any inconvenience this may have caused. _____

4 The flight out? Sardines – zombies – that says it all! _____

You didn't have any problem in identifying those, did you? No. 1 is a statement in straightforward terms appropriate from a report. This sort of style would also be suitable in a letter to a customer. However, no. 3, which is part of the letter of apology, is in a style which is not so appropriate in the report-writing we are looking at in this unit. We'll consider why later on.

I'm sure you recognized no. 2 as an internal memo: a brief 'telegraphic' style can be used as long as the meaning is clear. The slangy, chatty style of no. 4 belongs to that blue sky postcard!

**1.1**
**Get the message across**

In recent years, efforts have been made to present official information in a more attractive, readable and *understandable* way. Gobbledegook is still with us, unfortunately. But nowadays more attention is being paid to helping the public grasp the message.

Make *your* report understandable, easily digested. A report is not an essay which requires a flowing style. In a report a somewhat clipped style is acceptable. If in your report you had three points to get across, you might write:

'At this stage three points had to be considered:

1. availability;

2. size;

3. quality.'

To enlarge on these points you could make sub-headings and give further facts on each point:

'1 Availability

(a) Messrs R can supply from stock.

(b) Messrs S quote two months delivery.'

Long involved sentences mut be avoided: you cannot be sure the reader will stay with you all the way! For instance:

'The present forecasting has a tendency towards an inbuilt inaccuracy because it is based on the extrapolation process – this is, the examination and related assessment of previous performance, with an established estimated percentage increase/decrease (after allowing for inflation) – which does not take into consideration underlying and, in some cases, compensating deviations from past performances.'

Did you stay with this writer all the way? Really the statement should be split up into three or four separate sentences *and* simplified. But rather than spending time on it – just note the following warning.

**Project
Danger
Warning**

Long involved sentences
*can seriously obstruct understanding.*

**1.2
Facts, not drama**

Avoid 'emotive words'. We get used to seeing them in newspaper headlines, but they are totally out of place in a report. They may be colourful, but they are not *factual*.

● What is a *dramatic* fall in production?

● What is an *appalling* waste of material?

● What is a *huge* rise in absenteeism?

Your job is to interpret the facts for the reader in straightforward, unemotional language. Don't paint them with 'lurid' words that have no precise meaning. Let your reader judge whether a 10, 20 or 50 per cent fall or rise is *dramatic* or *huge*. State how much material is wasted and let your reader judge whether in the circumstances this is *appalling*.

**1.3
The likely
readership**

Consider what your likely readers know already. This will have a bearing both on the words you can use and the way you present the information.

Technical jargon is fine for quick communication between those in the particular technical circle. For those on the outside it is an unknown language and a cause of frustration.

A current example is the way in which people talk about computers. For those who are uninitiated into computers one of the biggest barriers to understanding is the racy jargon. It *sounds* like English, the words are familiar, but the way that they are used by the 'inner circle' makes no sense to the outsider.

A quite complicated concept can be understood by non-technical people provided it is expressed in words that are understandable to them.

# Activity 13

■ Time guide 5 minutes

Here is a situation where the words used would have to be carefully chosen.

Imagine you have a foreign visitor who learned a little English at school – just basic words, no slang or idioms. Before taking this visitor to your social club where there is a darts match on, you want to give him some idea of what a dartboard is and the method of scoring.

Make a note of the word or phases you would have to avoid using or explain very carefully.

_____

_____

_____

_____

On this action, I'm sure you thought up more than I did!

It strikes me that 'bull's eye', 'inner', 'outer', 'starting and ending on a double' could be a bit confusing for a foreigner with a limited knowledge of English.

Your starting point must be the present knowledge and vocabulary of the person you are addressing.

**1.4
Necessary technical terms**

In writing a report, all the time you have to bear in mind the present knowledge and vocabulary of likely readers. Where you need to use technical terms, you have three alternatives:

● put them in a context that makes the meaning obvious;

● give an explanation the first time the term occurs in the text;

● compile a 'Glossary of technical terms used' and put it in the Introduction or as an Appendix at the end of the report.

## 2     Writing in 'report' style

In this book you will find the words 'you' and 'we' and 'I'. The reason for this is that I wanted you to feel I was talking to you personally. There may be a number of different 'yous' (the publisher hopes to sell more than one copy!), but I am trying to communicate with the individual 'you' who is at present tackling a project, telling you all I can about how to carry it out and how to write a report. Very much a 'me' to 'you' communication.

Now, at the report-writing stage, I have to ask you to **do as I say** and **not** do as I have been doing in this book. I will try to explain why.

In the Planning section, 'the fly on the wall' approach was recommended. 'Look at the situation as if you were totally outside it.' In presenting your report you can maintain that 'outside the situation' feeling by writing in the 'third person'. It also helps to get across to the reader that your assessment of the situation is objective and unbiased.

Have a look at one or two examples.

- A supplier was contacted.
  (Rather than, *I* contacted a supplier.)

- It was found that quality had not been checked.
  (Not, *we* knew that there was no check on quality.)

- It is suggested that further tests be carried out.
  (Not, *I* think *you* should carry out further tests.)

It may help you to write in the 'third person' (report style), if you tell yourself that it is not you writing personally. It is a supervisor (or whatever your job title is) reporting to a senior.

# Activity 14

■ Time guide 5 minutes

Get used to the idea of writing in the third person by converting the following phases.

1  All of us in Formulation are on an 8 to 4 o'clock shift.

_____

_____

2  When our department gets the order sheet the first job is for me to write the total quantity in my book of daily totals.

_____

_____

3  What we had to do to speed up the process was ...

_____

_____

The way I converted these three is as follows:

1.  The Formulation personnel all work an 8 to 4 o'clock shift.

2.  When the order sheet reaches Dept X, the total quantity is entered in the daily totals book.

3.  To speed up the process it was necessary to ...

Don't worry if your wording is not exactly the same, so long as it sounds as if 'the fly on the wall' is making the report!

**2.1
Breaking the rules**

The comedian picks up a violin – or some other musical instrument – and produces ghastly sounds. Laughter rewards his efforts. In fact, the comedian is a good musician and can play the instrument well. He knows 'the rule' and how to break them to achieve a certain effect.

To break rules effectively we have to know what the rules are.

Once you know how to write in an impersonal style (and appreciate the sense of objectivity it conveys), you will realize that there may be times when the use of 'I' or 'we' can give a particular emphasis. An instance could be when making recommendations at the end of a report.

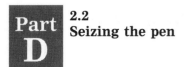

**2.2
Seizing the pen**

Whatever type of paper or card you have used for your notes, now is the time to start using A4 lined paper. It might be useful to have a ring binder with a minimum of two cardboard dividers (more if it helps you to feel well organized).

With just two dividers, the main part of your draft goes between the two, the preliminary pages go in front of the first divider and the appendices and back-up information go behind the other divider.

The middle bulk section is the tough part.

Very experienced writers will tell you that they dread the moment when they must start putting words on a blank sheet of paper! You feel the same ? You are in good company!

What follows now are suggestions to help you in compiling your written report. They are numbered and have headings. Read each one and then carry it out before moving on to the next.

Use simple, straightforward language and *think of the reader*.

## 3       Step-by-step suggestions

**3.1
The start**

At this stage don't concern yourself with finer points of presentation such as a title page. You need to get going on the actual writing. You are lucky, the first bit is ready: remember your TOR – what *you set out to do*? Clip them into your folder or rewrite them on to a clean A4 sheet and put that in front of the first divider.

# Activity 15

■ Time guide 30 minutes

While those who are using this book as an instruction manual are compiling their written report, you have a chance to revise and remind yourself of the relevant sections. TOR were covered in Part B, 3, so revise this section.

**3.2
Headings,
sub-headings, sections**

A long report that is not broken up into clear sections is hard work to read. Probably your project has already fallen into broad divisions in your mind.

If could help you at this stage to have a look at Appendix E (NEBSM project report layout). Consider this for a while, seeing how the evidence you have accumulated and your conclusions might fit into this format.

Now get your rough pad and draw up a skeleton plan of headings for *your* report. Your TOR should provide you with main heading captions. Don't worry if the ideal title for a section doesn't come to mind straight away. Get something down; it can be amended when you think up a better phrase.

When you are reasonably satisfied with the skeleton, transfer it to A4 paper and put it at the front of your folder so that you can tick off each section when it has been drafted.

**3.3
Background
circumstances**

What does the likely reader know of the *background circumstances*? The assessor knows nothing about you or the details of your organization. It would certainly help the NEBSM assessor if you gave some idea of what your organization is, its size and what its products or services are. The work of your own section and how it fits in could also be relevant.

For many readers it is helpful if there is an 'Introduction', to set the scene for what follows.

As an instance, take a project concerned with introducing a plated meals service for hospital patients. Those inside the hospital know its layout, but the outsider would find it hard to visualize without some information on such things as the kitchen and its situation, the number of wards, access to different storeys, and so on. Some of this background could be in words, some might be in the form of a diagram.

# Activity 16

■ Time guide 20 minutes

Try your hand at writing up a brief introduction to the organization you work for. Give some thought to possible diagrams that might help an outsider to visualize the layout of the section you work in.

**3.4
Any limitations**

The reader should be made aware of the scope of the project. This may mean explaining that certain aspects are **not** covered. Or perhaps you need to mention the reason why certain periods of time were chosen for analysis. You are defining the parameters.

# Activity 17

■ Time guide 20 minutes

Revise Part B, 2, on parameters.

**3.5
Methodology**

In reading a report it is often helpful to know **how** the author set about investigating and the way he or she investigated. Will this help **your** reader?

**3.6
The main body
of the report**

The present situation

In most cases an explanation of the situation as it existed when you started your investigation will form the opening of the main body of the report.

For instance, in the hospital meals project that I mentioned in point 3, a description of the present system of serving meals would be necessary, i.e. the way the meals are distributed from the kitchen to the patients.

The reader can then appreciate the factors involved in any proposed new system.

The facts

You worked hard, beavering away, accumulating evidence; *but* this does not mean that you have to describe in detail every wrong turning and every pot-hole you stumbled into on the way. Begin the pruning process. Cut out irrelevant material.

However, for your own sake, you should make the reader aware of the extent of your investigation. For instance, suppose you had compared products W, X, Y and Z. You will discuss in your report the relative merits and demerits of these four products. However, the fact that you also contacted the suppliers of T, U and V and found they could not supply in the required size or quality may be worth mentioning because it shows the extent of your search.

## Activity 18

Visuals

Is there a pictorial or graphic way that will communicate information more effectively than words?

Photographs can be a great aid to speedy assimilation of salient facts that would otherwise take a lot of words to describe.

In the section on 'Analysing the data' (Part C, 4) a number of types of charts and diagrams were mentioned (and illustrated).

Another very useful graphic device is the 'pie chart'. For instance, if you have used a questionnaire to obtain opinions, a series of 'pie charts', with 'shares of the pie' in different colours (or hatchings), will quickly convey the essence of the results to the readers.

Appendix D shows more detailed examples of these visuals which may help you to think 'graphically'.

## Activity 19

■ Time guide 15 minutes

Turn to Appendix D and check the way various graphs and diagrams are drawn. Also reread Part C, 4, on analysing data and 'thinking on paper'.

Appendices

You will have noticed that, from time to time in this study unit, supporting information has been put as an appendix at the back. The same applies to charts, diagrams, etc. Too many of these in the main written text can be like a dose of hiccups.

It is usually better not to interrupt the flow of your discussion, so the supporting data should be *referred to within the text*, but actually included at the back as Appendix A, Appendix B, etc. Only if it is vital to the understanding of a particular paragraph should the pictorial form of your evidence be included in the main body of the report.

Appendices should be lettered (or numbered) so that the readers can easily locate this supporting evidence if they wish. The appendices should be in the same sequence as they are referred to in the main text.

The discussion

As well as setting out the evidence, you are also putting all the facts into perspective. You give the reasoning that has led you to arrive at your conclusions. The 'Options' cards that you prepared earlier should help to marshall your ideas.

## Activity 20

■ Time guide 20 minutes
Revise Part C, 6.

**3.7**
**Conclusions**

Write down the conclusions you came to. This should not be difficult if you followed the practical suggestions in the 'Coming to conclusions' section of the previous chapter.

## Activity 21

■ Time guide 20 minutes

Revise Part C, 7.

**3.8**
**Recommendations**

These are the courses of action that you are able to recommend following your detailed investigation. Set them out clearly. Don't be woolly or vague. Have the courage of your convictions.

Any particular implications should be included (legal, safety, industrial relations and other human factors).

**3.9**
**Statement of cost and/or savings**

In some reports this may be appropriate as a separate item before or after the recommendations, or as an appendix.

**3.10**
**Numbering the report**

Giving letters and/or numbers to sections and paragraphs enables reference to be made to any part of the report.

As you have now written the main bulk of your report, it is time to read through your first draft. While doing so you should have a coloured pen in your hand so that you can add your numbering system. See Appendix F for the two systems commonly used.

**3.11**
**Summary or synopsis**

With a substantial piece of writing such as your project report, there should always be a summary or synopsis at the beginning. This gives an overall view of the whole report in 200 to 250 words. Each reader can then decide how much of the report he needs to read.

This summary should be done only when you are satisfied with your final draft. For the moment make a note on your time schedule that your summary has still to be written.

**3.12**
**Contents page**

This is another aid for the reader. Obviously you cannot put the page numbers in until the final copy is typed, but you can prepare the contents list. Your skeleton of headings is the basis for this.

Take a look at the contents pages of the study unit. Notice that the sub-section headings are clearly listed under their main section heading. Again we seek to make it as easy as possible for the reader's eye to take in information.

## Activity 22

■ Time guide 15 minutes

Turn to Part B. Try making out a contents page for this one part. Compare yours with the contents page at the front.

**3.13**
**Title page**

Have you thought up a title for your project? It should be brief, its purpose being to state the main topic. If you feel that a short title of two or three words is insufficient on its own, a sub-title can be added to give a more precise indication of what the report covers.

One sometimes see titles in the form of a question. (Do you remember that in the first 'Scene' the manager suggested that Joe's project title should be 'Layout – are we getting good value?'.)

**Part D**

This sort of title is a little journalistic; it is fine for an article in a publication where it is a device to catch the reader's eye and interest. Think carefully before using such a device. Consider whether it is appropriate for your report title, or even the sub-title.

Other items for the title page are:

Your name as the author

Job title (if the project is work-based)

National Examining Board for Supervisory Management
Certificate in Supervisory Management
Project Report

Date (month and year)

**3.14
Acknowledgements**

Now that you are within sight of the finishing post, take a few quiet moments to review the complete undertaking. Think about the people who have been helpful to you. Maybe your employer has given special facilities, or time off? Maybe an 'expert' has given advice? Maybe other departments have been especially co-operative?

Now you have an opportunity to acknowledge this help and support.

On a separate sheet, after the title page, you can express your appreciation. Put it in your own words, but something to the effect of 'The author would like to thank the following for their help (or advice or co-operation)'.

**3.15
Polishing, pruning
and improving**

Your first draft (complete with headings and sub-headings, appropriately numbered) is probably still in need of a lot of polishing, rewording and hacking.

Whenever you reread any section, make sure you are wearing your critic's hat. Pull no punches: be your own severest critic!

## 4     Layout and eye appeal

Do not base your ideas of appropriate layout on 'official' reports that are produced in thousands. Paper economy is not a major factor for your written report. What is vital is that each page should look attractive and not overfull. The layout should assist the reader to absorb the information.

## Activity 23

■ Time guide 5 minutes

Look at the following page layouts. Which of them would be a positive factor in getting the information across to the reader? At first glance, which page would your eye encourage you to read first? Now try to assess the good or bad features of each one before looking at my comments that follow.

|       |       |       |
|-------|-------|-------|
| A     | B     | C     |

|       |       |       |
|-------|-------|-------|
| D     | E     | F     |

A   The solid mass of words would be very off-putting. Single-line spacing, narrow margins and long paragraphs would make it difficult to read. To sum up – indigestible!

B   Double spacing and wider margins are easier on the eye. But the long paragraphs still make it look dull and monotonous.

C   Hurrah! There are some headings, but what a pity the rest of the heading line is used instead of being left as white space. Margins rather narrow.

D   This looks good. The headings stand out. The indented subsections clearly link the information they contain.

E   In comparison with the previous page, the narrow margins are obviously less pleasing. Note how the lines that overrun the right margin would almost make the attention fall off the edge of the page.

F   Quite pleasing to the eye. Good margins. Headings that stand out well. Although the bottom third of the written matter has a somewhat 'wodgy' look, the diagram above puts heart into the reader to tackle a stodgy paragraph.

**Part D**

**4.1**
**Getting the project into shape**

There is not *one* right format for reports any more than there is one right format for every sort of letter that is written. You have already had a good look at a format that would be acceptable for most NEBSM projects (Appendix E).

Consider your latest draft. Is your format satisfactory? Does it proceed logically from the TOR that set out your objectives? Try to look at it as if you had never seen it before.

**4.2**
**Author and editor combined**

You put yourself outside the situation when carrying out your project. You endeavoured to be impersonal – unbiased – when writing it up. However, the sheets of paper that represent all this work are very much part of you, the *author*.

Nevertheless, at this point you have to take another distancing step, this time right away from what you have written. You now have to become the *editor*.

As the editor, you are concerned with accuracy and completeness. You are editing with the reader in mind. You are cutting the waffle You are instructing the author to rewrite anything that is not absolutely clear and lucid. And, after the author has rewritten it, if you are not satisfied you will coldly order the author to draft that piece again, and again!

Gradually, between the two of you, *author* and *editor*, a final draft will appear.

**4.3**
**The final draft**

Now seek an outside opinion. The final draft of a NEBSM project should be vetted by the project (or course) tutor.

**4.4**
**The typescript**

Your typist (or word-processor operator) is entitled to have precise instructions on the following details.

● Margins: don't forget that the left-hand margin should be wide enough to allow for holding the sheets together.

● Spacing: NEBSM projects are usually typed in double spacing and should be on one side only of A4 paper.

● Number of copies required.

● Whether particular sections are to start on a fresh page. (Maybe you have already marked your text accordingly, preferably in a bold colour.)

Don't forget that if a chart has to be included *within* the main text, you must say what space needs to be left. Similarly, if you want anything typed (such as headings or labels) for items in the appendices, discuss with the typist how this is to be done.

Another point to agree with the typist is the numbering of the pages. These numbers have to be added to the contents page you have prepared.

Don't opt out of talking these matters through. It is *your* report. The final appearance is *your* responsibility. But, if you explain clearly how you want the final copy to look, you are more likely to get the co-operation you need.

When the typescript comes back to you – looking so beautiful you can hardly believe that you are the author – remember to say *thank you*. (Who knows – you might want another report typed one day?)

**4.5**
**The submission copy**

Try putting stick-out tags on the appendices. It makes it easier for the reader to flick over to the appropriate appendix.

What outer covers are you putting on? You need protection for your valuable work? Some people use looseleaf binders, but this can entail putting reinforcing stickers round the holes on every sheet. An alternative is to use a plastic slider for the spine with A4 carboard covers.

Many companies have some form of binding machine for making booklets. Office supplies retailers can sometimes offer the service.

Whatever form of binding you use, do make sure that everything can be read and that nothing is hidden by the way the report is held together. This can be a particular problem with charts and graphs that only just fit the page.

If any items in the Appendix are in 'landscape' rather the 'portrait' format, make sure that the top of the page is to the binder edge.

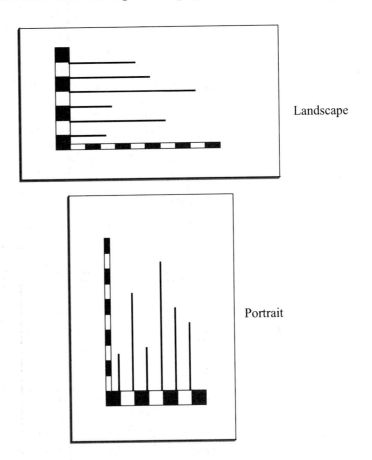

Landscape

Portrait

**4.6**
**A final scrutiny**

You, the author and editor, now have a final function to perform. You become the proof-reader. You read through to make sure there are no omissions and no typing errors. A serious omission would need some retyping perhaps, but it is acceptable to correct small errors neatly by hand with a black pen.

Check that everything is there and in the right order. Keep your concentration disciplined: don't let carelessness mar the final result.

# 5      Submitting the report

You have perserved. You have taken time and trouble. You have completed your project and the report. Now finish the task by doing all you can to see that your report is read by those who should read it.

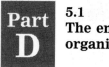
**5.1
The employing
organization**

An accompanying letter or memo addressed to a particular individual can draw attention to your project. Alternatively, request five minutes of a senior manager's time and hand over a copy personally.

Don't let the matter lapse. After an interval enquire (politely, of course) if any of the recommendations were of interest and, if so, the likelihood of their possible implementation.

**5.2
NEBSM assessment**

For work-based projects NEBSM requires confirmation from the employing organization of the validity of the technical or specialized content. Therefore, before your project report is delivered to the course tutor, it should be assessed by an appropriate person in the organization.

The observations of this person may be included in the copy submitted for NEBSM assessment. Alternatively the employer may wish to send such observations and comments directly to the tutor who will pass them on to the NEBSM assessor.

## 6      Summary

Your report is now complete, so this is the last opportunity for checking and ensuring that all is well. In fact this checklist is almost an insurance policy. An insurance is based on the principle of 'uberrima fides' (utmost good faith), you must be completely honest with yourself in answering the questions!

● Are your terms of reference stated clearly at the front of the report?

● Did you identify the problem and collect *all* the relevant facts?

● Is all the information set out clearly and logically?

● Have you eliminated all superfluous material?

● Have you used photographs, charts and diagrams to help in getting the message across?

● Does the evidence you have presented lead logically to the conclusions?

● Have you covered the cost aspects?

● Have you covered the human aspects?

● Are the recommendations set out clearly?

● Is your table of contents accurate?

● Are your appendices clearly labelled and easy to find?

● Is your summary complete and *concise*?

● Does the final report look attractive?

● Have you checked through the submission copy to make sure there are no errors in it?

● *Did you carry out your terms of reference?*

# APPENDICES

## 1     Table of contents

The NEBSM assessor will be looking at the following points in your project report.

● Presentation:

– is it well-presented and laid out?
– is it easy on the eye?
– is there a useful table of contents, a summary, a main theme with conclusions, recommendations, and appendices?
– is it likely to stimulate action?

● Investigation:

– how was it researched and how much detail is included?
– are the facts supported by evidence?
– how were problems overcome?

● Relevance:

– is all material relevant to the terms of reference?

● Completeness:

– has adequate information been collected?
– have all aspects, including finance and human factors, been covered?

● Charts etc.:

– what charting and graphic skills have been used?
– do they support the written word?

● Conclusions and recommendations:

– are they realistic?
– are they backed up by the information in the body of the report?

**Types of project**

- A survey of:
  - current practice (staffing, recruitment, shift systems, rotas, etc.);
  - paperwork/people involved (say, in the processing of orders from receipt to delivery);
  - the sales value of space in a retail business;
  - what improvements could be made.
- An experimental piece of work.
- A problem-solving exercise (to overcome a perceived difficulty).
- A 'new-equipment' project (plant, machines, vehicles, apparatus).
- A 'setting-up' project (new stores, canteen, social club).
- A 'moving' project (change of location with minimum hassle).
- An investigation to find 'a better way':
  - improved layout of machinery or work-stations;
  - more efficient work-flow;
  - improved methods;
  - improved service to public/customer;
  - better recording/filing systems;
  - improved public relations;
  - improved communication between specific sections (e.g. sales and production).
- A feasibility study for:
  - new plant/equipment;
  - new distribution pattern/area;
  - elimination of X;
  - addition of Y.
- A 'what if' study, i.e. assessment of likely outcome (e.g. centralization, decentralization, computerization).
- A cost-saving exercise, i.e. more output with the same input, or the same output with less input.
- A reorganization project (of a section or department, of work allocation).

- **Observation**

  Using your eyes and noting what is seen.

- **Experiment**

  This could be a 'laboratory-type' experiment or it could be trying something out, such as a method, a system, a machine, sometimes a series of trial runs. Careful notes and records are kept of what is tried and of the results.

- **Measuring**

  Counting, weighing, using a ruler or tape measure, skilled assessment. All recorded for subsequent comparison/evaluation.

- **Collection**

  Gathering together information on one subject from different sources. For example, from suppliers, users, customers, experts, people close to the information, old files, current files, libraries.

  Information may be requested by letter, memo, phone, telex, face-to-face talking.

- **Selection**

  Selecting information from one or several sources: for example, picking out relevant figures from computer print-outs.

- **Sampling**

  Investigating a random selection of a larger total number of items to gather specific data. The aim is to collect data which is representative of the whole.

- **Special techniques**

  Operational research, critical path analysis, work study, method study, etc.

- **Interviewing**

  Getting information from people by asking them questions face to face. This may be a matter of making an appointment with one individual with specialized knowledge. Or it could be a matter of interviewing several in order to get opinions. In the latter case it is advisable to prepare a list of questions beforehand for the sake of consistency.

- **Questionnaire**

  Getting information from people by asking them to indicate answers to questions set out on paper.

**Where to research**

● **Libraries**

Be as precise as possible about what you are seeking, then go and get the librarian's help. Try to go at a not-too-busy time. You may be astonished at what information is available from and through the library service. If the library you visit does not have a particular book, the librarian can often get it through a library-services network.

As well as a wide range of books, including encyclopaedias, directories, yearbooks, they have maps, atlases, gazetteers, technical journals, magazines, newspapers. They also have government publications, digests and abstracts of statistics, British and other countries' standards, etc.

● **Records kept by the business**

As well as financial accounting records and correspondence and personnel records, most businesses keep departmental records for some time: clock cards, overtime records, stock records, orders in and out, job sheets, estimates, etc.

**Graphics – every picture should tell a story**

This Extension includes a few ideas that may encourage you to think visually.

Remember that:

● visuals must have a title or label so that the reader knows what is being portrayed;

● graphs (always) and other charts (usually) should include an indication of scale so that the reader is made aware of 'how much' is portrayed.

The following types of visuals are illustrated in this extension:

● organization charts

● bar charts

● pie charts

● graphs, maps and matrices

Organization charts

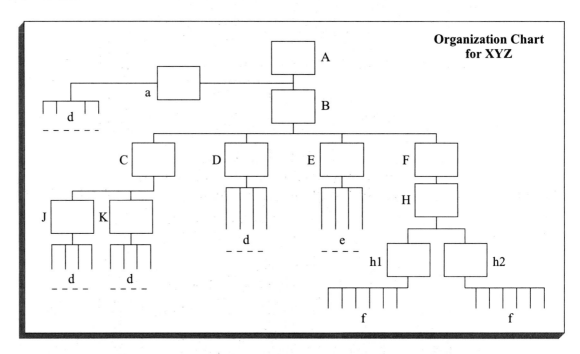

This form of organization chart is widely used. It indicates relationships and the responsibility for others by showing the spans of control from top to bottom.

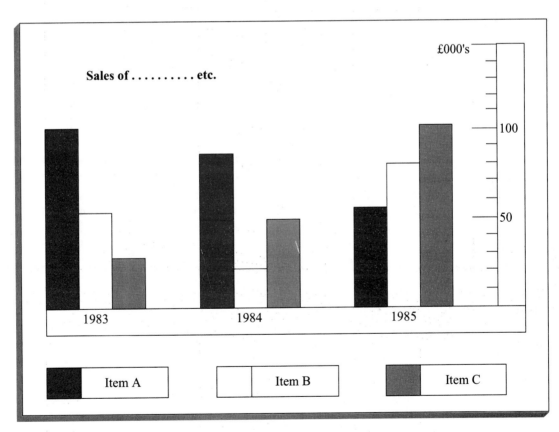

The bar chart above is an enlargement of that shown on page 38.

This chart compares 3 items over 3 years (see page 41 for text that could apply).

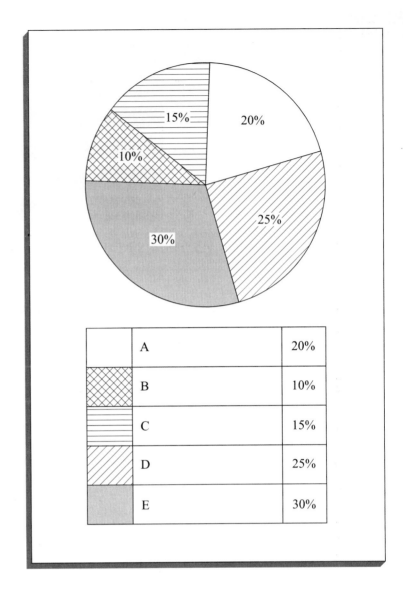

Pie charts can be used to show comparative shares or portions of a whole. This particular chart has slices ranging from 10% to 30% with the idea that *you* might find it useful as a guide (tracing on an overlay of thin paper). It would be easy to divide sections to obtain 5%, $12\frac{1}{2}$% and so on.

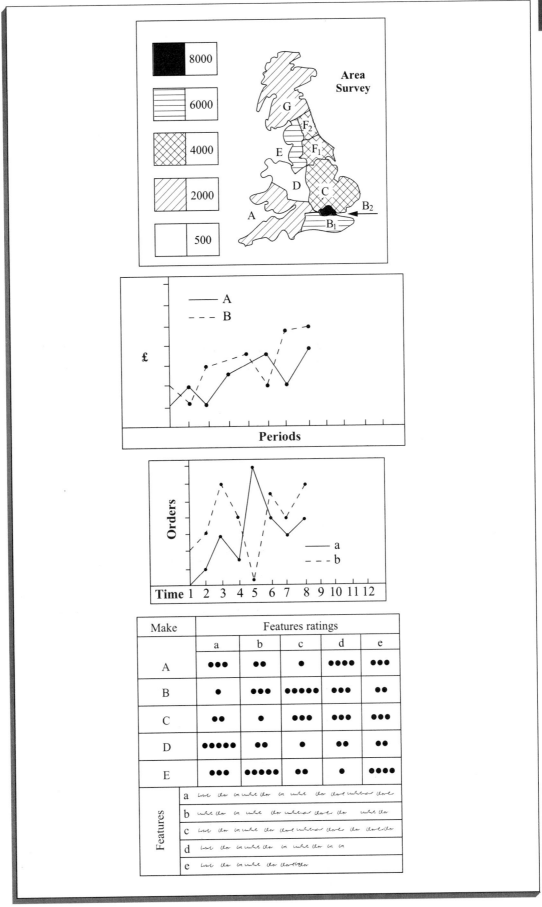

These are enlargements of those shown on pages 37, 38 and 39.

**NEBSM Project report layout**

The layout that follows is intended to give you guidance on the essentials of a well-presented project report. There are many possible variations. The chosen form will depend on what *you* are putting across.

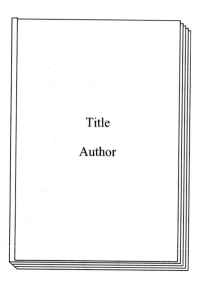

Front cover

The front cover is a practical means of protection for the report.

It also contributes to the initial impression made on the reader.

Often a number of project reports are being handled together, so there should be some identification of title and author.

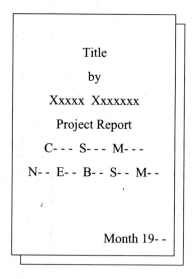

Title page

Title – a concise indication of the subject with, optionally, a sub-title to give a wider indication of subject matter.

Name of author. Job title (if a work-based project).

Project Report
Certificate in Supervisory Management
National Examining Board for Supervisory Management

Month and year.

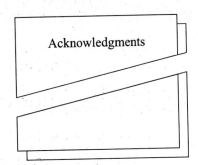

Acknowledgements

An opportunity to express formal appreciation: for help received, for special co-operation, for time given or allowed, etc.

Contents

|   |              | Page |
|---|--------------|------|
| 1 | Summary      | 1    |
| 2 | Introduction | 2    |
|   | 2.1 xxxxxxxxx | 3   |
|   | 2.2 xxxxx    | x    |
|   |              |      |
| 3 | xxxxxxx      |      |
|   | 3.1 xxxxx    | x    |
|   | 3.2 xxxxxxx  | x    |
|   | 3.3 xxxxxxxx | x    |
|   | 3.4 xxxxx    | xx   |

Table of contents

The headings and sub-headings of each section are set out. Indenting the sub-headings helps the eye of the reader.

Page numbers are inserted when the report is complete.

Appendices should be listed and numbered (or lettered) in the order in which they are referred to in the main report.

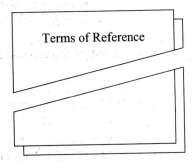

Terms of reference

These may be set out on a separate page or they may be incorporated in the title page or included in the summary; but beware of cramming a page to the point where readability is lost.

Summary

Summary
(or synopsis)

This is written last, of course.

It is the report in miniature and summarizes the essentials, including the recommendations.

The purpose is to give the reader in 200/300 words the main substance of the report that follows.

Introduction

Introduction

This is to prepare the reader for what follows. It may include some or all of these.

● Definition of problem

● Background/circumstances/history

● Assumptions/limitations/parameters

● Definitions and explanations

● Glossary of terms – if many words used are likely to be unfamiliar to some readers, include a glossary either at the beginning or as the first appendix.

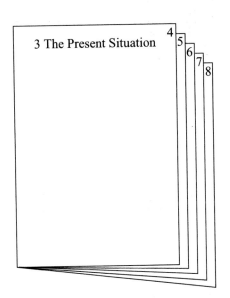

3 The Present Situation

Main body of
the report

This often commences with an analysis of the existing situation. It may continue with sections such as:

problems in present situation;

methods of investigation; or

plan of action.

The reader is made aware of the investigation that was undertaken. The facts obtained are set down and then analysed.

Possible solutions to the problem are discussed, together with their implications.

Costs and human factors are considered.

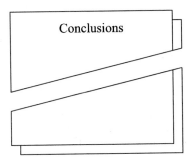

Conclusions

Conclusions

Deductions are drawn based on logical reasoning.

Alternatives must be weighed and evaluated and this will lead to ...

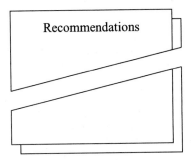

Recommendations

Recommendations

These are the author's proposals for the situation investigated. They need not be dramatic or revolutionary: they may even confirm that the present situation is best.

Key implications of the proposals should be mentioned.

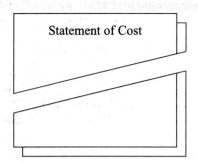

Statement of cost

A statement of cost and/or saving that would result from the recommendations needs to be set out clearly in the report. It could be included before or after the recommendations, or possibly on the same page.

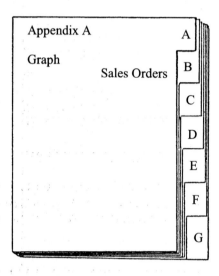

Appendices

These are for tables, charts, graphs, samples, examples, leaflets, etc. – any supporting evidence and information which would interrupt the flow of the 'discussion' if included in the main body of the report.

They are not for irrelevant information put in to build up bulk.

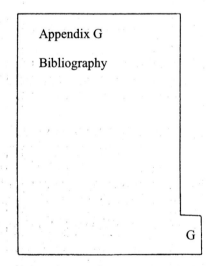

Bibliography

This could be one of the Appendices or a separate item before the Appendix.

If any information has been drawn from books, other published material, or reports, its source should be given so that the original material could be located if the reader so wished.

**Numbering a report**

There are two systems commonly used:

● letter/number;

● decimal.

Letter/number system

Alternate letters and numbers are used to indicate descending order of magnitude:

I  Major division ... then II, III, IV, etc.
    A  Chapter ... B, C, D
        1  Subject ... 2, 3, 4
            (a)  Section ... (b), (c), (d)

If you wanted sub-sections you would use small roman numerals ... (i), (ii), (iii), (iv) and so on.

It would also be acceptable to miss out the big roman numeral and start with capital letters for the major divisions. Chapter headings would then be numbered 1, 2, 3 and the subjects would then be indicated by (a), (b), (c) and so on.

Use what feels comfortable and natural, but try to keep the alternate letter/number sequence.

Decimal numbering system

Some organizations insist on this system for all reports. It works like this.

Chapters are 1, 2, 3, etc.

In Chapter 1, subjects are 1.1, 1.2, 1.3, etc.

To indicate that subject 1.1 has a number of sections to it, these are numbered 1.11, 1.12, 1.13, etc.

In Chapter 2, subjects are 2.1, 2.2, etc., and sections become 2.12, 2.13, and so on.

Further divisions are made by adding another digit, so that sub-sections of section 3 of the 4th subject in Chapter 5 would become 5.431, 5.432, 5.433, etc.

**'Bristolmove' list**

The following is the list prepared by Helen for her meeting with her brother on Saturday. It is based on her 'brainstorming session', which she then got typed out. It is not in any particular priority order.

| | Project - Bristolmove | Who to do |
|---|---|---|
| | Date leaving old house . . . . New address . . . . | |

**Advise:**
| Electricity Board | – arrange meter reading on last day |
| Gas Board | – likewise |
| Brit. Telecom | – likewise |
| Water Authority | – pay apportionment of rates |
| Local Rating Auth. | – ? apportionment of rates paid |

**Check for Bristol house:**
Electricity connected
Gas ditto?
Brit. Telecom re installation of new phone?
Change of phone no. cards with new number if OK

**Inform** (zero + 7):
Milk - bread - newspapers - cancel deliveries after zero +1

**Re post:** GPO form for change of address.
Suggest pay for 12 months' redirection service.

**Removal services:**
Get quotes from two removal firms. Arrange contract with one making best offer. Get from them (zero + 15) tea chests, cardboard boxes, etc. for us to pack small items, crockery, glass, etc. Check timing - how long to load - to go 250 miles - likely time of arrival at new house next day.

**Freezer:** How do removal people cope with this? Full chest must weigh a ton. Content valuable - can't give away. Find answer.

**Get:** Good supply plastic bags/covers for clothes on hangers, linen, etc.

**Plans:** Get copy of plans for room layout and size from Bristol builders.
Also window dimensions and what, if any, curtain fittings supplied.

**Check:** Existing curtains. Any usable without alteration? Can some be altered? Possibly need hooks. Fit ready to put up.

**Planning move in:**
Make copies of layout plan. Pam to use these to work out where she wants what to go in new house. When she has got it right she can make out a list on cards (one for each room) and mark up the final plan. (Note - destroy trial efforts.) Each room on plan to be marked up with a letter. Every item (furniture - carpets - tea-chests - cartons, etc.) to be labelled according to Pam's what-goes-where list. Get supply of tie-on and adhesive labels. (Colour-coding might help removal men on arrival at Bristol).

**Note re Pam:**
She must not be involved in packing or other tiring work. There is plenty she can do without wearing herself out.

**Help?** Possible extra help for packing tea-chest, etc. Zero + 8 or 9. (Pam's mother? My daily help?)

**Note:** All newspapers to be saved from now on for packing.
? get roll of corrugated cardboard?

| | |
|---|---|
| Labelling: | Start S.A.P. with furniture. Can remain in situ until zero day. Don't leave to last minute, else mistakes likely. Pam to make out labels. Others of us can do affixing. Remember items in garage and garden shed. |

**Change of address:**

Prepare list of people to be notified.                                             Pete/Pam
? run off set message on office copier or get cards printed?
Address cards according to list.                                                    Pam
Get stamps and stamp cards ready for posting.                                      Pam

**House keys:**

Keys to be returned to old firm. Pete say how. (Post? Collection?)
If post prepare large stamped addressed envelope and stick on wall by front door.

**Insurances:**

Advise insurers of change of address. Arrange cover for contents at new house. ? In transit? ? Building cover?

**Medical services:**

Pam to advise present doctor of move. Register with Bristol medical practice ASAP - and have check-up there.

| | |
|---|---|
| Zero + 8: | Start packing tea-chests and boxes. |
| Zero + 7: | Order delivery of mini-skip (to dispose of 4 years' accumulated rubbish). Those items not wanted but sound - how about Garage Sale? |

**Between zero + 2 and + 6:**

Will Pete need to go to Bristol to see new employers?
To stop Pam becoming overstressed with the chaos of moving out, suggest Pete takes her to Bristol so she focuses on moving *in*. Book into small hotel/guest house near new home. Pete to return to base.

**In Bristol – Pam's responsibilities:**

To take it steady!! Get orientated in new area - local shops, etc. Get house keys. Post change of address cards. Find new medical centre (doctor) and register. Order: milk - bread - newspaper deliveries. Organise: tea and sandwiches for when removal men arrive.

| | |
|---|---|
| Zero + 1: | Peter to doss down at my flat. He'll need good night's sleep. Also kitchen can be cleared and bed-linen taken off. |
| Zero day: | Take large tea-pot from flat and nosh to keep us all sustained. (If cooker going - look out all my vacuum flasks.) Make sure all kitchen and bedroom items loaded on last. Thus first off - survival kit for first night in new house in case removal van arrives late in day. Alternative - book that night at Pam's small hotel. Check old house. Lock up and return keys to the company. |

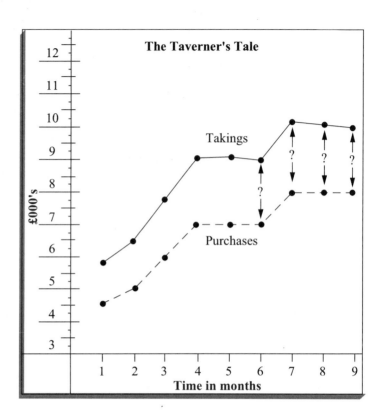

Graphs can look very different according to the scale that is used. So don't worry if yours is rather different from this one. The main thing is that it should show the relationship between the takings line and the purchases line – and the same trends that can be seen on the one here. Have you noticed that the two lines are gradually getting further apart up to month 6 – and then begin to get closer.

Let's take up the story again. In that sort of business, with the stock staying roughly steady. The difference between the two lines is a broad indication of gross profit. The question you would have to ask Philip is, 'what difference is there in the sort of things you've been selling since month 6. Are there any changes in the business?'

If Philip replies, 'Just being busier and selling more of everything, and month 5 was when I took on extra help in the bar', warning bells might start ringing and you could find yourself saying, 'Well, Philip, you may find that the extra help you took on is helping itself!'

Pilferage could be the reason for the change in the picture – Philip's purchases are replacing some stock that has gone – but not been paid for. Alternatively not all the takings have been put in the till.

Philip said, 'I've got a nasty feeling that something's not right, know what I mean?'

Maybe he'll have learned from your graph that if he wants to stay in business he'd better get to know what his figures mean – and not wait for his accountant to tell him when it's too late to remedy matters!